D1308536

Life of Christ

INVITED TO LOVE

Student Workbook

WP Wheaton Press
Train. Equip. Reflect.

Life of Christ
Student Workbook

© 2010, 2012
Published by Wheaton Press
Wheaton, Illinois

www.WheatonPress.com

All rights reserved. No part of this publication may be reproduced, stored in a retrieval system, or transmitted in any form or by any means-for example, electronic, photocopy, recording-without the prior written permission of the publisher. The only exception is brief quotations in printed reviews.

ISBN–13: 978–0615695235
ISBN–10: 061569523X

1. Christian Education – Discipleship 2. Spiritual Formation – Discipleship. 3. Life of Christ – Education. 4. Nonfiction-Religion and Spirituality-Christian Life. 5. Nonfiction-Spiritual Growth-Christ-centered.

Copyright and Trademark Standard

thetrustlist™ © 2000, 2011, 2012 Matthew Dominguez, thetrustlist.com. All rights reserved. Used by permission.

The Examine Assessment™ copyright 1996, 2004, 2010, 2012 Wheaton Press™. All Rights Reserved. Free to download, copy, distribute, repost, reprint and share, for non-commercial use provided it appears in its entirety without alteration with copyright information and WheatonPress.com both visible and unaltered.

Scripture quotations are from The Holy Bible, English Standard Version® (ESV®), copyright 2001 by Crossway, a publishing ministry of Good News Publishers. Used by permission. All rights reserved.
Scripture taken from the Holy Bible, NEW INTERNATIONAL VERSION®.
Copyright 1973, 1978, 1984 by Biblica, Inc.
Scripture taken from The Holy Bible: International Standard Version (ISV),
Copyright 1998, 2008. All rights reserved.
Scripture quotations are taken from the Holy Bible, New Living Translation, copyright ©1996, 2004, 2007. Used by permission of Tyndale House Publishers, Inc., Carol Stream, Illinois 60188. All Rights Reserved.
New American Standard Bible Copyright © 1960, 1962, 1963, 1968, 1971, 1972, 1973, 1975, 1977, 1995 by The Lockman Foundation, La Habra, Calif. All rights reserved.
Scripture taken from the Contemporary English Version®
Copyright © 1995 American Bible Society. All rights reserved.
GOD'S WORD® is a copyrighted work of God's Word to the Nation. Quotations are used by permission. Copyright 1995 by God's Word to the Nations. All rights reserved.

This document contains proprietary research, copyrighted materials, and literary property of Engaged Solutions™ (EngagedSchools™). Wheaton Press™, Engaged Solutions™, Engaged Churches™, Engaged Teams™, Engaged Church Summit™, Equip 4Ministry™, Equip 4Teams™, Strengths-Based Ministry Teams™, Engaged Marriage™, Engaged Generation™, Engaged Schools™ are all trademarks of Engaged Solutions™. All other trademarks noted are property of their respective owners.

Accordingly, international and domestic laws and penalties guaranteeing patent, copyright, trademark, and trade secret protection safeguard the ideas, concepts, and recommendations related within this document.

Contact the publisher for discounted copies for partner schools and receive free resources and training for teachers. Learn more at WheatonPress.com or email WheatonPress@gmail.com

Who do you say that I AM?

Mark 8:29, NIV

Life of Christ

Equipping Students to Reflect Christ

	STEP ONE	STEP TWO	STEP THREE	STEP FOUR
Growth Emphasis	An Emphasis on Believing	An Emphasis on Following	An Emphasis on Loving	An Emphasis on Going
Essential Questions	1. What does a healthy, mature follower of Christ believe? 2. How does a healthy, mature follower of Christ live?	3. How do I grow as a healthy, mature follower of Christ? 4. How do I equip others to grow as healthy, mature followers of Christ?	5. Who do others say Jesus is? 6. Who do I say Jesus is?	7. What do I believe? 8. Why do I believe? 9. How will I communicate to others?
Essential Outcomes	Understand and articulate Christ-centered **beliefs**	Develop authentic Christ-centered **values**	Develop and articulate a Christ-centered **vision**	Develop a clear Christ-centered personal **mission**
Courses	**Foundations of Faith**	**Spiritual Formations** **Leadership, Evangelism, & Discipleship**	**Life of Christ** **Philosophy & Theology**	**Doctrine & Apologetics** **Christ & Culture**

    ©2010, 2012. Wheaton Press™ All Rights Reserved.

Class Overview

Course Essential Questions

1. Who is Jesus?

2. What is my response to His invitation?

Unit Essential Questions

1. #Jesus: Who do others say that He is?

2. #Perspective: How do I view Jesus?

3. #Messiah: Is Jesus the Messiah?

4. #Divine: Is Jesus fully God?

5. #Human: Was Jesus fully human?

6. #Atonement: Why did Jesus die on a cross?

7. #Resurrected: Did Jesus rise from the dead?

8. #Returning: What will happen when Jesus returns?

9. #Response: Who do I say that He is?

Course Description

This class will focus on inviting students to become friends of Christ. Students will examine and apply the concept of Christ's role as our prophet, priest, and king. Students will gain an understanding of Jesus as the fulfillment of prophecy and will not only understand His place in history, but also His relevance to our lives today. Ultimately, the hope is that Jesus' life and message will transform students' lives as they gain a greater understanding of who Christ is in their individual lives, and personalize their response to Him.

Key Doctrines

A. Jesus is—and claimed to be—the only God (Christian theism, Trinity).

B. Jesus is our prophet, priest, and king.

C. Jesus was 100% fully God (hypostatic union).

D. Jesus was 100% fully human (hypostatic union, *kenosis*).

E. Jesus lived a sinless life among us (incarnation).

F. Jesus became the penal substitutionary atonement for our sin (justification).

G. Jesus rose from the dead, and is currently sitting at the right hand of the Father as our mediator and intercessor in His exalted glory (Christology).

H. Jesus will return (eschatology).

I. Jesus calls us into relationship with Him (soteriology, sanctification).

J. Jesus calls us to follow in His steps (sanctification, missiology).

Unit 1   #Jesus: Who do others say that He is?

1. What is the learning goal for this workbook, *The Life of Christ*?

2. What do I currently know about Jesus?

3. What is the Gospel Project?

4. What is the context for the essential question for this class?

5. What does John 1–2 reveal about Christ?

6. How does our culture view Christ?

Unit 2   #Perspective: How do I view Jesus?

1. What is the tri–perspective view of Jesus?

2. How does my perspective of Jesus influence my relationship with Him?

3. What is the application of the tri–perspective view of Christ to my life?

4. What does John 3–8 reveal about Christ?

5. What are the faith foundations of a complete monist?

Unit 3   #Messiah: Is Jesus the Messiah?

1. What does the Bible tell us about the Messiah?

2. Does Jesus meet the requirements to be the Messiah?

3. How does the central theme of Scripture center on Christ?

4. What does John 9–15 reveal about Jesus?

Unit 4   #Divine: Is Jesus fully God?

1. Why does it matter whether or not Jesus was fully divine?

2. What do other religions believe about the divinity of Jesus Christ?

3. Did Jesus claim to be God?

4. Why was Jesus crucified?

5. What is significant about the word *Elohim*?

6. What does John 16–21 reveal about Christ?

Unit 5   #Human: Was Jesus fully human?

1. Was Jesus fully human?

2. What is Gnosticism?

3. What is the *kenosis* and why does it matter?

4. If Jesus was fully human, how could He live a perfect life?

5. What does Matthew 1–7 reveal about Jesus?

     ©2010, 2012. Wheaton Press™ All Rights Reserved.

Unit 6   #Atonement: Why did Jesus die on a cross?

1. What happened physically to Christ on the cross?

2. What happened spiritually through the sacrifice of Christ on the cross?

3. What happened theologically through the atoning work of Christ?

4. How are the perfect love and perfect wrath of God fulfilled through the death of Christ on the cross?

5. Did Jesus go to hell after He died?

Unit 7   #Resurrected: Did Jesus rise from the dead?

1. What do I believe about the resurrection of Christ from the dead?

2. Is it reasonable to believe that Jesus rose from the dead?

3. What biblical and circumstantial evidence exists that Jesus rose from the dead?

4. What non-Christian, historical evidence exists that Jesus rose from the dead?

5. Can I articulate a clear apologetic for the resurrection of Christ from the dead?

Unit 8   #Returning: What will happen when Jesus returns?

1. How does the life of Christ fit into the eternal plan of God?

2. Where is Jesus now?

3. How does the return of Christ fit into the eternal plan of God?

4. What will He do when He returns?

5. How should my beliefs influence my current life?

Unit 9   #Response: Who do I say that He is?

1. What is the meaning of worship?

2. What functional saviors compete for prominence in my life?

3. What will be my response to the invitation of Christ?

4. How will I articulate what I have learned?

©2010, 2012. Wheaton Press™ All Rights Reserved.

Gospel Project
Gospel check due dates

Gospel check 1	John 1–2	Due _____
Gospel check 2	John 3–8	Due _____
Gospel check 3	John 9–15	Due _____
Gospel check 4	John 16–21	Due _____
Gospel check 5	Matthew 1–7	Due _____
Gospel check 6	Matthew 8–14	Due _____
Gospel check 7	Matthew 15–21	Due _____
Gospel check 8	Matthew 22–28	Due _____
Gospel check 9	Luke 1–7	Due _____
Gospel check 10	Luke 8–14	Due _____
Gospel check 11	Luke 15–21	Due _____
Gospel check 12	Luke 22–24	Due _____
Gospel check 13	Mark 1–7	Due _____
Final project	Mark 8–16	Due _____

 ©2010, 2012. Wheaton Press™ All Rights Reserved.

#Jesus

Life of Christ

Unit Essential Questions

1. What is the desired outcome of this class?

2. What can I expect during and after this class?

Unit Learning Objectives

A. To understand the essential questions, learning objectives, and expectations of this class

B. To identify my personal learning needs

C. To develop a personalized learning plan for this class

D. To understand the significance of this class and the course assignments in the overall scheme of life

Unit Learning Assessments

1. Expectations for growth personal reflection handout

2. The Global Student Assessment

3. Final exam pre–assessment

4. Personal spiritual formation assessment

Daily Essential Questions

1. What is the learning goal for this workbook, *Life of Christ*?

2. What do I currently know about Jesus?

3. What is the Gospel Project?

4. What is the context for the essential question of this class?

5. What does John 1–2 reveal about Christ?

6. How does our culture view Christ?

 ©2010, 2012. Wheaton Press™ All Rights Reserved.

My Expectations

1.   The name that I like to be called is (nickname) _____.

2.   The reason that I'm taking this class is because (other than because it's required):

3.   One thing that I'm looking forward to in this class is:

4.   Two things that I want to learn in this class include:

     1.

     2.

5.   One goal that I have for myself this year is:

6.   One thing that my teacher could pray for me about this semester would be:

7.   My relationship with Jesus up to this point in my life could best be described as:

©2010, 2012. Wheaton Press™ All Rights Reserved.

My Best Class Ever

Part I. Individual Response

1. What was the best class that I have ever been a part of?

2. What made it the best class ever?

3. What did the teacher do to make it the best class ever?

4. What did I do to make it the best class ever?

5. What did the other students in the class do to make it the best class ever?

Part II. Pair and Share

1. Three ideas I really liked that I heard from someone else include:

2. One thing I think we should commit to, as a class, to make this the best class ever is:

 ©2010, 2012. Wheaton Press™ All Rights Reserved.

Name: _____   Period: _____

1. What are the three primary offices that are woven through the Old Testament and fulfilled in Jesus Christ?

    A.

    B.

    C.

2. Who does Paul claim was the greatest Old Testament prophet?

3. How many synoptic Gospels are in the orthodox New Testament canon?

4. How much of the Bible was prophetic at the time of its original writing?

5. Over how long of a period of time was the Old Testament written?

6. How would you explain to a friend the prophecies about Christ in the Old Testament that have yet to be fulfilled?

7. When can we expect the remaining Old and New Testament prophecies about Christ to be fulfilled?

8. Why does it matter if Jesus was or was not fully divine? Explain in your own words.

©2010, 2012. Wheaton Press™ All Rights Reserved.

9. How would a lack of full divinity affect Christ's roles from the tri–perspective view of Christ? Explain the implications for each role specifically:

    •

    •

    •

10. At what point in His life and ministry did Jesus become fully divine?

11. What Old Testament name is the name *Jesus* derived from?

12. What does the name *Jesus* mean?

13. Roughly how many years ago was Jesus born?

14. What does the title *Christ* mean?

   ©2010, 2012. Wheaton Press™ All Rights Reserved.

List a few specific core beliefs about the nature and person of Christ for the following cults or religious movements:

15. Emergent Christians:

16. Jehovah's Witnesses:

17. Mormonism:

18. Unitarian Universalism:

19. Scientology:

20. Buddhism:

21. Islam:

22. Followers of Mahatma Gandhi:

©2010, 2012. Wheaton Press™ All Rights Reserved.

Further questions

23. When Jesus refers to himself as the "Son of Man," what is it a reference to?

24. You are sitting at a coffee shop with a friend. During the discussion he says, "Jesus never claimed to be God, so why would you believe that he is?" What is your response?

    A.   Is your friend's statement true? Why or why not?

    A.   If you claim that your friend's statement is false, where would you go in Scripture to show what you believe? (explain your response)

25. With regard to the claims of Jesus, C.S. Lewis wrote that Jesus could only be one of three things. Lewis concluded that the third was Lord. What are the first two?

    A.

    A.

26. Define the word *incarnation*.

 ©2010, 2012. Wheaton Press™ All Rights Reserved.

27. Some groups who professed heresies concerning the person of Christ include the Ebionites, Gnostics, Arians, and Apollinarians. Explain how each heresy views Christ:

28. Explain why the Gnostic and Arian view of Jesus is not compatible with Scripture:

29. What New Testament book was written in large part to defend that Jesus was fully human, with a real physical body?

30. If Jesus had not been fully human, what aspect of the tri–perspective view of Christ would be null and void?

31. What vital doctrine of orthodox faith regarding the person of Christ was discussed, debated, and ratified during the Council of Chalcedon?

32. Define the Greek word *hypostasis* and explain why it is significant.

33. Define the Greek word *kenosis* and explain why it is significant.

34. Define the term *Hypostatic Union* and explain why it is significant.

35. Where in Scripture is the key passage that describes the *kenosis* found?

Define the following words from a theological perspective:

36. Propitiation:

37. Expiation:

38. Atonement:

39. Penal Substitutionary Atonement:

40. Substitution:

41. Imputation:

42. Justification:

43. Sanctification:

44. Glorification:

45. Forbearance:

46. Scapegoat:

47. Day of Atonement:

48. Reconciliation:

    ©2010, 2012. Wheaton Press™ All Rights Reserved.

Further questions

49. List three ways the Apostle Paul uses the word *saved* in the New Testament. Give Scripture references to support your answers.

     A.

     B.

     C.

50. List three ways that Christ's death fulfilled the Old Testament sacrificial system. Give Scripture references to support your answers.

     A.

     B.

     C.

51. Did Jesus have to die? Why or why not? Explain your answer with Scripture.

52. How is both the perfect love and perfect wrath of God displayed through the cross of Christ?

©2010, 2012. Wheaton Press™ All Rights Reserved.

53. What term was created to describe the amount of pain an individual experienced during the process of crucifixion? What does the word literally mean?

54. Give three historical pieces of evidence that Jesus rose from the dead.

    A.

    B.

    C.

55. Give three circumstantial pieces of evidence that Jesus rose from the dead.

    A.

    B.

    C.

56. Give three biblical references that state that Jesus rose from the dead.

    A.

    B.

    C.

57. Where is Jesus today? Defend your answer using Scripture.

 ©2010, 2012. Wheaton Press™ All Rights Reserved.

Reflection

What are my initial thoughts and impressions after taking the pre–assessment?

Questions for discussion and consideration:

1. What do I already know, and what do I need to learn?

2. How do I grow to reflect Christ in every area of my life if I don't know who He is?

3. How do I equip others to grow to reflect Christ if I don't know who He is?

©2010, 2012. Wheaton Press™ All Rights Reserved.

Life of Christ

Reflection

What is the Gospel Project?

"Take the helmet of salvation and the sword of the Spirit, which is the word of God."
Ephesians 6:17, NIV

"For the word of God is alive and active. Sharper than any double–edged sword, it penetrates even to dividing soul and spirit, joints and marrow; it judges the thoughts and attitudes of the heart."
Hebrews 4:12, NIV

 ©2010, 2012. Wheaton Press™ All Rights Reserved.

Examine ™

SPIRITUAL FORMATION TOOL

ChristCenteredDiscipleship.com

Everyone ought to examine themselves before they eat of the bread and drink from the cup.
1 Corinthians 11:28, NIV

WP Wheaton Press
Read. Respond. Reflect.™

Where are you?

Read. Respond. Reflect.

Directions: *Read through the verses below and highlight or underline any words or phrases that seem to reflect or resonate with where you are at.*

Skeptic. Presented with the person of Christ and the gospel multiple times, I demonstrate disinterest or unbelief.

"Even after Jesus had performed so many signs in their presence, they still would not believe in him." John 12:37, NIV

Characteristics: Calloused heart, dull ears, closed eyes.

"[F]or this people's heart has grown callous, their ears are dull of hearing, they have closed their eyes." Matthew 13:15a, WEB

Christ's Next-Step Invitation: Repent. Believe.

"Then he began to denounce the cities in which most of his mighty works had been done, because they didn't repent." Matthew 11:20 ,WEB

Growth Barrier: A lack of spiritual understanding.

"When anyone hears the message about the kingdom and does not understand it, the evil one comes and snatches away what was sown in their heart. This is the seed sown along the path." Matthew 13:19, NIV

Spiritual Need: A change of mind and heart initiated by the Holy Spirit, a loving and praying friend.

"He said to them, 'This kind can come out by nothing, except by prayer and fasting.'" Mark 9:29, WEB

"As for you, you were dead in your transgressions and sins, in which you used to live when you followed the ways of this world and of the ruler of the kingdom of the air, the spirit who is now at work in those who are disobedient." Ephesians 2:1-2, NIV

Seeker. Questioning, with a desire to learn more about Jesus.

"He answered, 'And who is he, sir? Tell me, so that I may believe in him.'" John 9:36, ISV

Characteristics: A ready heart, open ears, questions with an interest to learn more about Jesus.

"Again, the next day, John was standing with two of his disciples, and he looked at Jesus as he walked, and said, 'Behold, the Lamb of God!' The two disciples heard him speak, and they followed Jesus. Jesus turned, and saw them following, and said to them, 'What are you looking for?' They said to him, 'Rabbi' (which is to say, being interpreted, Teacher), 'where are you staying?' He said to them, 'Come, and see.' They came and saw where he was staying, and they stayed with him that day. It was about the tenth hour." John 1:35-39, WEB

Christ's Next-Step Invitation: Repent. Believe.

"Now after John was taken into custody, Jesus came into Galilee, preaching the Good News of God's Kingdom, and saying, 'The time is fulfilled, and God's Kingdom is at hand! Repent, and believe in the Good News.'" Mark 1:14-15, WEB

Growth Barrier: A lack of clear presentation and understanding of the gospel, a lack of invitation.

"How, then, can people call on someone they have not believed? And how can they believe in someone they have not heard about? And how can they hear without someone preaching?" Romans 10:14, ISV

Spiritual Need: A clear gospel presentation and an invitation to believe and receive salvation.

"But to all who did receive him, who believed in his name, he gave the right to become children of God." John 1:12, ESV

Believer. Presented with the gospel I believe.

"He said, 'Lord, I believe!' and he worshiped him." John 9:38, WEB

Characteristics: Seed begins to germinate, shallow soil, little or no roots.

Other seeds fell on rocky ground, where they did not have much soil, and immediately they sprang up, since they had no depth   of soil, but when the sun rose they were scorched. And since they had no root, they withered away. Matthew 13:5-6

Christ's Next-Step Invitation: Follow.

"And he said to them, 'Follow me, and I will make you fishers of men.'" Matthew 4:19, ESV

Growth Barrier: Lack of roots, lack of knowledge, testing, trouble, persecution.

"These in the same way are those who are sown on the rocky places, who, when they have heard the word, immediately receive   it with joy. They have no root in themselves, but are short-lived. When oppression or persecution arises because of the word,   immediately they stumble. " Mark 4:16-17, WEB

Spiritual Need: Prayer, roots, knowledge, biblical teaching, time, worship and someone to walk with them.

"Like newborn infants, long for the pure spiritual milk, that by it you may grow up into salvation." 1 Peter 2:2, ESV

"So then, just as you received Christ Jesus as Lord, continue to live your lives in him, rooted and built up in him, strengthened in   the faith as you were taught, and overflowing with thankfulness." Colossians 2:6-7, NIV

"We continually ask God to fill you with the knowledge of His will through all the wisdom and understanding that the Spirit gives,   so that you may live a life worthy of the Lord and please Him in every way: bearing fruit in every good work, growing in the   knowledge of God, being strengthened with all power according to His glorious might so that you may have great endurance and   patience, and giving joyful thanks to the Father, who has qualified you to share in the inheritance of His holy people in the   kingdom of light." Colossians 1:9-12, NIV.

The Reflect Assessment™ copyright 1996, 2004, 2010, 2012 Wheaton Press™. All Rights Reserved. Free to download, copy, distribute, repost, reprint and share, for non-commercial use provided it appears in its entirety without alteration with copyright information and WheatonPress.com both visible and unaltered. For more information and complete Scripture, use copyright information available at WheatonPress.com.

Follower. Growing in faith and love; deepening roots and knowledge; struggling with thorns, trials, forgiveness, doubt, and perseverance.

"By this all people will know that you are my disciples, if you have love for one another." John 13:35, ESV

Characteristics: Beginning to push through the soil, struggling with thorns and weeds.

"Others fell among thorns. The thorns grew up and choked them." Matthew 13:7, WEB

"And calling the crowd to him with his disciples, he said to them, 'If anyone would come after me, let him deny himself and take up his cross and follow me.'" Mark 8:34, ESV

Christ's Next-Step Invitation: Deny self; pick up cross; trust, obey, and love Christ and others.

"Then Jesus said to his disciples, "If anyone desires to come after me, let him deny himself, and take up his cross, and follow me." Matthew 16:24, WEB

Growth Barrier: Thorns, worries of this life, doubt, deceitfulness of wealth, comfort, self and self-will.

"Others are those who are sown among the thorns. These are those who have heard the word, and the cares of this age, and the deceitfulness of riches, and the lusts of other things entering in choke the word, and it becomes unfruitful." Mark 4:18-19

Spiritual Need: Deny self; trials; endurance, perseverance, time, small group relationships, and accountability.

"Consider it pure joy, my brothers and sisters, whenever you face trials of many kinds, because you know that the testing of your faith produces perseverance. Let perseverance finish its work so that you may be mature and complete, not lacking anything." James 1:2-4, NIV

"Through him we have also obtained access by faith into this grace in which we stand, and we rejoice in hope of the glory of God. Not only that, but we rejoice in our sufferings, knowing that suffering produces endurance, and endurance produces character, and character produces hope." Romans 5:2-4, ESV

"These have come so that the proven genuineness of your faith—of greater worth than gold, which perishes even though refined by fire—may result in praise, glory and honor when Jesus Christ is revealed." 1 Peter 1:7, NIV

Friend. Marked by obedient love for Christ and others; may wrestle with isolation, complacency and accountability.

"You are my friends if you do what I command you." John 15:14, ESV

Characteristics: Good soil, obedience to Christ, fruit, growing faith, increasing love and perseverance in trials.

"We ought always to thank God for you, brothers and sisters, and rightly so, because your faith is growing more and more, and the love all of you have for one another is increasing. Therefore, among God's churches we boast about your perseverance and faith in all the persecutions and trials you are enduring." 2 Thessalonians 1:3-4, NIV

Christ's Next-Step Invitation: Love, obey, go, teach.

"If you love me, you will keep my commandments." John 14:15, ESV

"Jesus came to them and spoke to them, saying, 'All authority has been given to me in heaven and on earth. Go, and make disciples of all nations, baptizing them in the name of the Father and of the Son and of the Holy Spirit, teaching them to observe all things that I commanded you. Behold, I am with you always, even to the end of the age.' Amen." Matthew 28:18-20

Growth Barrier: Complacency, fear, pride, lack of vision and lack of equipping.

"Then he said to his disciples, 'The harvest indeed is plentiful, but the laborers are few.'" Matthew 9:37, WEB

"How, then, can people call on someone they have not believed? And how can they believe in someone they have not heard about? And how can they hear without someone preaching?" Romans 10:14, ISV

Spiritual Need: Vision, continued obedience, equipping, empowerment, continued spurring and accountability within community.

"…to equip his people for works of service, so that the body of Christ may be built up until we all reach unity in the faith and in the knowledge of the Son of God and become mature, attaining to the whole measure of the fullness of Christ." Eph 4:12-13

"As for you, brothers, do not grow weary in doing good." 2 Thessalonians 3:13, ESV

"Let us continue to hold firmly to the hope that we confess without wavering, for the one who made the promise is faithful. And let us continue to consider how to motivate one another to love and good deeds, not neglecting to meet together, as is the habit of some, but encouraging one another even more as you see the day of the Lord coming nearer." Hebrews 10:23-25, ISV

Fisherman. Reflecting Christ and reproducing fruit of righteousness and good works.

"Because we have heard of your faith in Christ Jesus and of the love you have for all God's people—the faith and love that spring from the hope stored up for you in heaven and about which you have already heard in the true message of the gospel that has come to you. In the same way, the gospel is bearing fruit and growing throughout the whole world—just as it has been doing among you since the day you heard it and truly understood God's grace." Colossians 1:4-6, NIV

Characteristics: Good soil, fruitfulness, harvest, influence, reflecting Christ.

"Others fell on good soil, and yielded fruit: some one hundred times as much, some sixty, and some thirty." Matthew 13:8, WEB

Christ's Next-Step Invitation: Teach others.

"Therefore, as you go, disciple people in all nations, baptizing them in the name of the Father, and the Son, and the Holy Spirit, teaching them to obey everything that I've commanded you." Matthew 28:19-20a, ISV

Growth Barrier: Complacency, fear, pride, lack of vision, lack of equipping, weariness.

"Let's not get tired of doing what is good, for at the right time we will reap a harvest—if we do not give up." Galatians 6:9, ISV

"Think about the one who endured such hostility from sinners, so that you may not become tired and give up." Hebrews 12:3,

Spiritual Need: Perseverance, humility, faithfulness, accountability, reliable people.

"It gave me great joy when some believers came and testified about your faithfulness to the truth, telling how you continue to walk in it." 3 John 3, NIV

"And what you have heard from me in the presence of many witnesses entrust to faithful men who will be able to teach others also." 2 Timothy 2:2, ESV

Examine™: Spiritual Formation Planning Tool
More resources available at WheatonPress.com

Directions: Answer the following seven questions using the words or phrases that you highlighted or underlined.

1. Where am I?
Skeptic. When presented with the gospel, I do not believe.
Seeker. Questioning, with a desire to learn more about Jesus.
Believer. Presented with the gospel I chose to believe.
Follower. Growing in faith, love, and roots; struggling with thorns, trials and perseverance.
Friend. Marked by obedient love for Christ and others.
Fisherman. Reflecting Christ and bearing fruit of righteousness and good works.

2. Where would I like to be in 6 months?
Skeptic. When presented with the gospel, I do not believe.
Seeker. Questioning, with a desire to learn more about Jesus.
Believer. Presented with the gospel I chose to believe.
Follower. Growing in faith, love, and roots; struggling with thorns, trials and perseverance.
Friend. Marked by obedient love for Christ and others.
Fisherman. Reflecting Christ and bearing fruit of righteousness and good works.

3. What invitation do I need to respond to in order to take my next step?
Skeptic. Repent.
Seeker. Repent. Believe.
Believer. Follow.
Follower. Deny self. Pick up cross. Obey. Love Christ and others.
Friend. Love. Obey. Go.
Fisherman. Teach others.

4. What barriers will I face?
Skeptic. Calloused heart, deaf ears, closed eyes.
Seeker. Lack of clear testimony. Lack of invitation.
Believer. Lack of root. Testing. Trouble. Persecution.
Follower. Thorns. Worries of this life. Deceitfulness of wealth. Comfort. Self.
Friend. Complacency. Fear. Lack of vision. Lack of equipping.
Fisherman. Complacency. Fear. Lack of vision. Lack of equipping. Weariness.

5. What spiritual needs do I have?
Skeptic. Prayer. Repentance, A believing friend.
Seeker. Receive. Believe. Salvation.
Believer. Prayer. Roots. Knowledge. Teaching. Worship. Time.
Follower. Deny self. Trials. Endurance. Perseverance. Time. Small group relationships and accountability.
Friend. Vision. Continued obedience. Equipping. Opportunity. Empowerment. and accountability within community.
Fisherman. Perseverance. Faithfulness. Reliable people.

6. What steps will I take?

7. Who will I ask to hold me accountable?

The Reflect Assessment™ copyright 1996, 2004, 2010, 2012 Wheaton Press™. All Rights Reserved. Free to download, copy, distribute, repost, reprint and share, for non–commercial use provided it appears in its entirety without alteration with copyright information and WheatonPress.com both visible and unaltered. More information and complete Scripture use copyright information available at WheatonPress.com.

Christ and Culture Artifact
Interviews and Dialogue

Part I. Interviews

Directions:

Conduct a brief, two-question interview with three different people. Your assignment is simply to ask the following questions, listen, and record their answers:

1. How is Christ portrayed in our culture?

2. How has culture changed their perspective of Christ over the course of your life?

You will submit a paragraph summary for each of the three interviews that you conduct (three paragraphs total for the interview section).

Your fourth, final paragraph will be a brief description of your artifact (see part II below). Explain why you chose it and how it represents how culture portrays Christ.

NOTE:
- At least one person needs to be a family member, and at least one person needs to be a student who is not participating in this class (and preferably who is not a student at this school).
- This assignment would make a great "meal–time" discussion with your family.

Part II. Artifact

Directions:

Identify an artifact of how Christ is portrayed in our culture and bring it into class to share.

Part III. Class Discussion

Class Dialogue and Reflection

1. Based on our initial assessments, what do we currently know and what do we need to learn?

2. How is Christ being presented by our current culture?

1. How does culture influence our perspective of Christ?

2. How is our perspective of Christ currently influencing culture?

What does it mean to *hagah* (meditate)?
Word Study

Notes and Discussion

 ©2010, 2012. Wheaton Press™ All Rights Reserved.

What does it mean to *halak*?
Passage Study: Mark **8**

Notes and Discussion

What does John 1 reveal about Christ?
Word Study: John 1

Notes and Discussion

 ©2010, 2012. Wheaton Press™ All Rights Reserved.

What does John 1 reveal about Christ?

#Perspective

Life of Christ

Unit Essential Questions

1. What is the tri–perspective view of Christ?

2. How is my current perspective of Christ influencing my relationship with Jesus?

Unit Learning Objectives

A. To understand Christ's role as our prophet, priest, and king

B. To understand the various applications of the tri–perspective view of Christ on everyday life

C. To examine our life and assess our current perspective of Christ

D. To examine and understand the perspective of Christ's family on His claim to be the Messiah

Unit Learning Assessments

1. Tri–perspective reflection paper

2. Tri–perspective reflection presentation

Daily Essential Questions

1. What is the tri–perspective view of Jesus?

2. How does my perspective of Jesus influence my relationship with Him?

3. What is the application of the tri–perspective view of Christ to my life?

4. What does John 3–8 reveal about Christ?

 ©2010, 2012. Wheaton Press™ All Rights Reserved.

What is the tri–perspective view of Christ?

Notes and Discussion

©2010, 2012. Wheaton Press™ All Rights Reserved.

What is the application of the tri–perspective view of Christ to everyday life?

Notes and Discussion

 ©2010, 2012. Wheaton Press™ All Rights Reserved.

What is the application of the tri–perspective view of Christ to everyday life?

Notes and Discussion

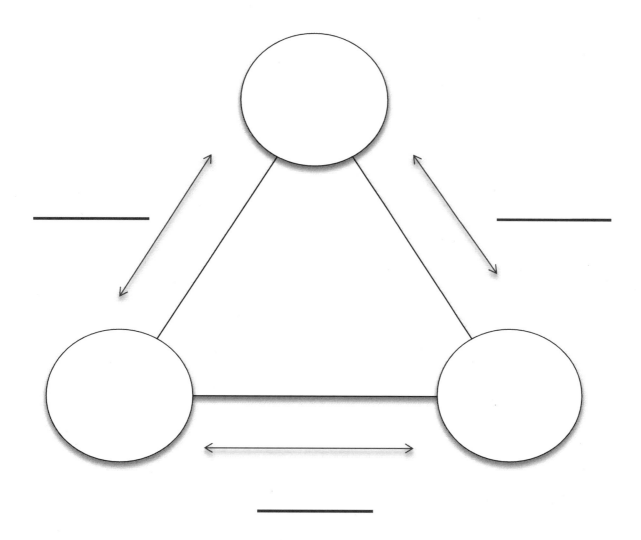

©2010, 2012. Wheaton Press™ All Rights Reserved.   35

What does John 3 reveal about Christ?

Notes and Discussion

 ©2010, 2012. Wheaton Press™ All Rights Reserved.

What does John 3 reveal about Christ?

What does John 7 reveal about Christ?

Notes and Discussion

Essential Question

How is my perspective of Christ influencing my reflection of Jesus?

Learning Goal

To articulate understanding and application of the concept of the tri–perspective view of Christ

Part I. Reflection paper

Purpose: The student will use this paper to demonstrate an understanding of the concepts and application of the tri–perspective view of Christ in his or her life.

Directions: Write a 1–2 page reflection paper that demonstrates your understanding of the concepts behind the tri–perspective view of Christ and answers the four questions below, using the guidelines for a one–page paper.

- Do you most easily identify with Jesus as a prophet, priest or king? (Demonstrate your understanding of why).
- How might this be affecting your relationship with Jesus? (Use your answer to demonstrate your understanding of the concepts involved).
- What perspective are you lacking?
- What steps will you take to develop a fuller, more complete understanding of the person and work of Jesus?

Students will demonstrate understanding of the following concepts as articulated through the assigned reading and classroom lectures:

The ministry of Jesus Christ as prophet, priest, and king;

A. The ministry of Jesus Christ as prophet, priest and king.
- Jesus the prophet: *Ministry is to proclaim the Word of God.*
  Jesus not only proclaimed the written Word of God, but was literally the incarnate, living Word of God.
- Jesus the priest: *Ministry is to mediate between God and man.*
  Jesus is the superior High Priest.
  Jesus is the superior sacrifice.
  Jesus is the superior intercessor.
- Jesus the king: *Ministry is to rule over all material and immaterial worlds.*

A. Application of the tri–perspective view of Christ
   Religious Legalism: Jesus = Prophet + King – Priest
   Emergent Liberalism: Jesus = Priest + King – Prophet
   Evangelical Moralism: Jesus = Prophet + Priest – King

Part II. Presentation

Directions: Students will present their reflection papers in class. Presentations will be approximately 2–4 minutes long. Students will be graded on content, preparedness, attentiveness to other presenters, and how well the presentation articulates an understanding of the concepts.

   ©2010, 2012. Wheaton Press™ All Rights Reserved.

Gospel Check Insights
Notes and Discussion

©2010, 2012. Wheaton Press™ All Rights Reserved.   39

Gospel Check Insights
Notes and Discussion

 ©2010, 2012. Wheaton Press™ All Rights Reserved.

#Messiah

Life of Christ

Unit Essential Questions

1. Did Jesus fulfill the Old Testament prophecies from Isaiah concerning the Messiah?

2. Is Jesus the Messiah?

Unit Learning Objectives

A. To understand the connections between the Old and New Testaments regarding the Messiah

B. To examine the prophecies in the book of Isaiah regarding the Messiah

C. To examine events in the New Testament regarding the life of Christ

D. To formulate a personal apologetic regarding the reasonableness of Christ being the Messiah

Unit Learning Assessments

1. Prophecy project

2. Prophecy project reflection paper

Daily Essential Questions

1. What does the Bible tell us about the Messiah?

2. Does Jesus meet the requirements to be the Messiah?

3. How does the central theme of Scripture center on Christ?

4. What does John 9–15 reveal about Jesus?

    ©2010, 2012. Wheaton Press™ All Rights Reserved.

Is Jesus the Messiah?

Why does biblical prophecy matter?

Biblical prophecy is one of the ways that we can identify the Messiah.

Moses, David, Daniel, Ezekiel, Isaiah, and others prophesied about the future birth, life, death, resurrection, and return of the Messiah. Some of it would be fulfilled within the next 300 years, other parts over the period of the next 3,000. The odds of being able to "foretell" over 300 exact events concerning this single person, and then having Him fulfill each one, is nothing short of miraculous.

The Bible is full of miraculous prophecies: words spoken by humans through the inspiration of the Holy Spirit of God. In the next few class periods, you will be examining 116 specific prophecies from the book of Isaiah regarding the future Messiah.

Examine for yourself:

Read Deuteronomy 18:21–22 and, in your own words, write what Moses says about whether or not we know if a message has been spoken by the Lord.

What does this mean? What are the implications of the words of Moses?

©2010, 2012. Wheaton Press™ All Rights Reserved.

Old Testament Prophecies Fulfilled by Jesus Christ

Prophecy	Description	Fulfillment
1. Gen 3:15	Seed of a woman (virgin birth)	Gal 4:4-5; Matt 1:18
2. Gen 3:15	He will bruise Satan's head	Heb 2:14; 1 John 3:8
3. Gen 5:24	The bodily ascension to heaven illustrated	Mark 16:19
4. Gen 9:26-27	The God of Shem will be the Son of Shem	Luke 3:36
5. Gen 12:3	Seed of Abraham will bless all nations	Gal 3:8; Acts 3:25-26
6. Gen 12:7	The Promise made to Abraham's Seed	Gal 3:16
7. Gen 14:18	A priest after the order of Melchizedek	Heb 6:20
8. Gen 14:18	King of peace and righteousness	Heb 7:2
9. Gen 14:18	The Last Supper foreshadowed	Matt 26:26-29
10. Gen 17:19	Seed of Isaac (Gen 21:12)	Rom 9:7
11. Gen 22:8	The Lamb of God promised	John 1:29
12. Gen 22:18	As Isaac's seed, will bless all nations	Gal 3:16
13. Gen 26:2-5	The Seed of Isaac promised as the Redeemer	Heb 11:18
14. Gen 28:12	The Bridge to heaven	John 1:51
15. Gen 28:14	The Seed of Jacob	Luke 3:34
16. Gen 49:10	The time of His coming	Luke 2:1-7; Gal 4:4
17. Gen 49:10	The Seed of Judah	Luke 3:33
18. Gen 49:10	Called Shiloh or One Sent	John 17:3
19. Gen 49:10	Messiah to come before Judah lost identity	John 11:47-52
20. Gen 49:10	Unto Him shall the obedience of the people be	John 10:16
21. Ex 3:13-15	The Great "I AM"	John 4:26; 8:58
22. Ex 12:5	A Lamb without blemish	Heb 9:14; 1 Pet 1:19
23. Ex 12:13	The blood of the Lamb saves from wrath	Rom 5:8
24. Ex 12:21-27	Christ is our Passover	1 Cor 5:7
25. Ex 12:46	Not a bone of the Lamb to be broken	John 19:31-36
26. Ex 15:2	His exaltation predicted as Yeshua	Acts 7:55-56
27. Ex 15:11	His Character-Holiness	Luke 1:35; Acts 4:27

 ©2010, 2012. Wheaton Press™ All Rights Reserved.

Prophecy	Description	Fulfillment
28. Ex 17:6	The Spiritual Rock of Israel	I Cor 10:4
29. Ex 33:19	His Character-Merciful	Luke 1:72
30. Lev 1:2-9	His sacrifice a sweet smelling savor unto God	Eph 5:2
31. Lev 14:11	The leper cleansed-Sign to priesthood	Luke 5:12-14; Acts 6:7
32. Lev 16:15-17	Prefigures Christ's once-for-all death	Heb 9:7-14
33. Lev 16:27	Suffering outside the Camp	Matt 27:33; Heb. 13:11-12
34. Lev 17:11	The Blood-the life of the flesh	Matt 26:28; Mark 10:45
35. Lev 17:11	It is the blood that makes atonement	Rom. 3:23-24; I John 1:7
36. Lev 23:36-37	The Drink-offering: "If any man thirst"	John 7:37
37. Num 9:12	Not a bone of Him broken	John 19:31-36
38. Num 21:9	The serpent on a pole-Christ lifted up	John 3:14-18; 12:32
39. Num 24:17	Time: "I shall see him, but not now."	John 1:14; Gal 4:4
40. Deut 18:15	"This is of a truth that prophet"	John 6:14
41. Deut 18:15-16	"Had you believed Moses, you would believe me."	John 5:45-47
42. Deut 18:18	Sent by the Father to speak His word	John 8:28-29
43. Deut 18:19	Whoever will not hear must bear his sin	Acts 3:22-23
44. Deut 21:23	Cursed is he that hangs on a tree	Gal 3:10-13
45. Joshua 5:14-15	The Captain of our salvation	Heb 2:10
46. Ruth 4:4-10	Christ, our kinsman, has redeemed us	Eph 1:3-7
47. I Sam 2:35	A Faithful Priest	Heb. 2:17; 3:1-3, 6; 7:24-25
48. I Sam 2:10	Shall be an anointed King to the Lord	Matt 28:18; John 12:15
49. 2 Sam 7:12	David's Seed	Matt 1:1
50. 2 Sam 7:13	His Kingdom is everlasting	2 Pet 1:11
51. 2 Sam 7:14a	The Son of God	Luke 1:32; Rom 1:3-4
52. 2 Sam 7:16	David's house established forever	Luke 3:31; Rev 22:16
53. 2 Ki 2:11	The bodily ascension to heaven illustrated	Luke 24:51
54. I Chr 17:11	David's Seed	Matt 1:1; 9:27
55. I Chr 17:12-13	To reign on David's throne forever	Luke 1:32-33
56. I Chr 17:13	"I will be His Father, He...my Son."	Heb 1:5
57. Job 9:32-33	Mediator between man and God	I Tim 2:5
58. Job 19:23-27	The Resurrection predicted	John 5:24-29
59. Psa 2:1-3	The enmity of kings foreordained	Acts 4:25-28
60. Psa 2:2	To own the title, Anointed (Christ)	John 1:41; Acts 2:36

©2010, 2012. Wheaton Press™ All Rights Reserved. 45

Life of Christ

Prophecy	Description	Fulfillment
61. Psa 2:6	His Character-Holiness	John 8:46; Rev 3:7
62. Psa 2:6	To own the title King	Matt 2:2
63. Psa 2:7	Declared the Beloved Son	Matt 3:17; Rom 1:4
64. Psa 2:7-8	The Crucifixion and Resurrection intimated	Acts 13:29-33
65. Psa 2:8-9	Rule the nations with a rod of iron	Rev 2:27; 12:5; 19:15
66. Psa 2:12	Life comes through faith in Him	John 20:31
67. Psa 8:2	The mouths of babes perfect His praise	Matt 21:16
68. Psa 8:5-6	His humiliation and exaltation	Heb 2:5-9
69. Psa 9:7-10	Judge the world in righteousness	Acts 17:31
70. Psa 16:10	Was not to see corruption	Acts 2:31; 13:35
71. Psa 16:9-11	Was to arise from the dead	John 20:9
72. Psa 17:15	The resurrection predicted	Luke 24:6
73. Psa 18:2-3	The horn of salvation	Luke 1:69-71
74. Psa 22:1	Forsaken because of sins of others	2 Cor 5:21
75. Psa 22:1	"My God, my God, why have You forsaken me?"	Matt 27:46
76. Psa 22:2	Darkness upon Calvary for three hours	Matt 27:45
77. Psa 22:7	They shoot out the lip and shake the head	Matt 27:39-44
78. Psa 22:8	"He trusted in God, let Him deliver Him"	Matt 27:43
79. Psa 22:9-10	Born the Savior	Luke 2:7
80. Psa 22:12-13	They seek His death	John 19:6
81. Psa 22:14	His blood poured out when they pierced His side	John 19:34
82. Psa 22:14-15	Suffered agony on Calvary	Mark 15:34-37
83. Psa 22:15	He thirsted	John 19:28
84. Psa 22:16	They pierced His hands and His feet	John 19:34-37; 20:27
85. Psa 22:17-18	Stripped Him before the stares of men	Luke 23:34-35
86. Psa 22:18	They parted His garments	John 19:23-24
87. Psa 22:20-21	He committed Himself to God	Luke 23:46
88. Psa 22:20-21	Satanic power bruising the Redeemer's heel	Heb 2:14
89. Psa 22:22	His Resurrection declared	John 20:17
90. Psa 22:27-28	He shall be the governor of the nations	Col 1:16
91. Psa 22:31	"It is finished"	John 19:30; Heb 10:10-12, 14, 18
92. Psa 23:1	"I am the Good Shepherd"	John 10:11; 1 Pet 2:25
93. Psa 24:3	His exaltation predicted	Acts 1:11; Phil 2:9

    ©2010, 2012. Wheaton Press™ All Rights Reserved.

Prophecy	Description	Fulfillment
94. Psa 30:3	His resurrection predicted	Acts 2:32
95. Psa 31:5	"Into Your hands I commit My spirit"	Luke 23:46
96. Psa 31:11	His acquaintances fled from Him	Mark 14:50
97. Psa 31:13	They took counsel to put Him to death	Matt 27:1; John 11:53
98. Psa 31:14-15	"He trusted in God, let Him deliver him"	Matt 27:43
99. Psa 34:20	Not a bone of Him broken	John 19:31-36
100. Psa 35:11	False witnesses rose up against Him	Matt 26:59
101. Psa 35:19	He was hated without a cause	John 15:25
102. Psa 38:11	His friends stood afar off	Luke 23:49
103. Psa 38:12	Enemies try to entangle Him by craft	Mark 14:1; Matt 22:15
104. Psa 38:12-13	Silent before His accusers	Matt 27:12-14
105. Psa 38:20	He went about doing good	Acts 10:38
106. Psa 40:2-5	The joy of His resurrection predicted	John 20:20
107. Psa 40:6-8	His delight is the will of the Father	John 4:34; Heb 10:5-10
108. Psa 40:9	He was to preach the Righteousness in Israel	Matt 4:17
109. Psa 40:14	Confronted by adversaries in the Garden	John 18:4-6
110. Psa 41:9	Betrayed by a familiar friend	John 13:18
111. Psa 45:2	Words of grace come from His lips	John 1:17; Luke 4:22
112. Psa 45:6	To own the title, God or Elohim	Heb 1:8
113. Psa 45:7	A special anointing by the Holy Spirit	Matt 3:16; Heb. 1:9
114. Psa 45:7-8	Called the Christ (Messiah or Anointed)	Luke 2:11
115. Psa 45:17	His name remembered forever	Eph 1:20-21; Heb. 1:8
116. Psa 55:12-14	Betrayed by a friend, not an enemy	John 13:18
117. Psa 55:15	Unrepentant death of the betrayer	Matt 27:3-5; Acts 1:16-19
118. Psa 68:18	To give gifts to men	Eph 4:7-16
119. Psa 68:18	Ascended into Heaven	Luke 24:51
120. Psa 69:4	Hated without a cause	John 15:25
121. Psa 69:8	A stranger to own brethren	John 1:11; 7:5
122. Psa 69:9	Zealous for the Lord's House	John 2:17
123. Psa 69:14-20	Messiah's anguish of soul before crucifixion	Matt 26:36-45
124. Psa 69:20	"My soul is exceeding sorrowful"	Matt 26:38
125. Psa 69:21	Given vinegar in thirst	Matt 27:34
126. Psa 69:26	The Savior given and smitten by God	John 17:4; 18:11

©2010, 2012. Wheaton Press™ All Rights Reserved.

Life of Christ

Prophecy	Description	Fulfillment
127. Psa 72:10-11	Great persons were to visit Him	Matt 2:1-11
128. Psa 72:16	The corn of wheat to fall into the Ground	John 12:24-25
129. Psa 72:17	Belief on His name will produce offspring	John 1:12-13
130. Psa 72:17	All nations shall be blessed by Him	Gal 3:8
131. Psa 72:17	All nations shall call Him blessed	John 12:13; Rev 5:8-12
132. Psa 78:1-2	He would teach in parables	Matt 13:34-35
133. Psa 78:2b	To speak the Wisdom of God with authority	Matt 7:29
134. Psa 80:17	The Man of God's right hand	Mark 14:61-62
135. Psa 88	The Suffering and Reproach of Calvary	Matt 27:26-50
136. Psa 88:8	They stood afar off and watched	Luke 23:49
137. Psa 89:27	Firstborn	Col 1:15-18
138. Psa 89:27	Emmanuel to be higher than earthly kings	Luke 1:32-33
139. Psa 89:35-37	David's Seed, throne, kingdom endure forever	Luke 1:32-33
140. Psa 89:36-37	His character-Faithfulness	Rev 1:5; 19:11
141. Psa 90:2	He is from everlasting (Micah 5:2)	John 1:1
142. Psa 91:11-12	Identified as Messianic, used to tempt Christ	Luke 4:10-11
143. Psa 97:9	His exaltation predicted	Acts 1:11; Eph 1:20
144. Psa 100:5	His character-Goodness	Matt 19:16-17
145. Psa 102:1-11	The Suffering and Reproach of Calvary	John 19:16-30
146. Psa 102:25-27	Messiah is the Preexistent Son	Heb 1:10-12
147. Psa 109:25	Ridiculed	Matt 27:39
148. Psa 110:1	Son of David	Matt 22:42-43
149. Psa 110:1	To ascend to the right-hand of the Father	Mark 16:19
150. Psa 110:1	David's son called Lord	Matt 22:44-45
151. Psa 110:4	A priest after Melchizedek's order	Heb 6:20
152. Psa 112:4	His character-Compassionate, Gracious, et al	Matt 9:36
153. Psa 118:17-18	Messiah's Resurrection assured	Luke 24:5-7; 1 Cor 15:20
154. Psa 118:22-23	The rejected stone is Head of the corner	Matt 21:42-43
155. Psa 118:26a	The Blessed One presented to Israel	Matt 21:9
156. Psa 118:26b	To come while Temple standing	Matt 21:12-15
157. Psa 132:11	The Seed of David (the fruit of His Body)	Luke 1:32; Act 2:30
158. Psa 129:3	He was scourged	Matt 27:26
159. Psa 138:1-6	The supremacy of David's Seed amazes kings	Matt 2:2-6

 ©2010, 2012. Wheaton Press™ All Rights Reserved.

Prophecy	Description	Fulfillment
160. Psa 147:3-6	The earthly ministry of Christ described	Luke 4:18
161. Prov 1:23	He will send the Spirit of God	John 16:7
162. Prov 8:23	Foreordained from everlasting	Rev 13:8; I Pet 1:19-20
163. Song 5:16	The altogether lovely One	John 1:17
164. Isa 2:3	He shall teach all nations	John 4:25
165. Isa 2:4	He shall judge among the nations	John 5:22
166. Isa 6:1	When Isaiah saw His glory	John 12:40-41
167. Isa 6:8	The One Sent by God	John 12:38-45
168. Isa 6:9-10	Parables fall on deaf ears	Matt 13:13-15
169. Isa 6:9-12	Blinded to Christ and deaf to His words	Acts 28:23-29
170. Isa 7:14	To be born of a virgin	Luke 1:35
171. Isa 7:14	To be Emmanuel-God with us	Matt 1:18-23; I Tim 3:16
172. Isa 8:8	Called Emmanuel	Matt 28:20
173. Isa 8:14	A stone of stumbling, a Rock of offense	I Pet 2:8
174. Isa 9:1-2	His ministry to begin in Galilee	Matt 4:12-17
175. Isa 9:6	A child born-Humanity	Luke 1:31
176. Isa 9:6	A Son given-Deity	Luke 1:32; John 1:14; I Tim 3:16
177. Isa 9:6	Declared to be the Son of God with power	Rom 1:3-4
178. Isa 9:6	The Wonderful One, Peleh	Luke 4:22
179. Isa 9:6	The Counselor, Yaatz	Matt 13:54
180. Isa 9:6	The Mighty God, El Gibor	I Cor 1:24; Titus 2:3
181. Isa 9:6	The Everlasting Father, Avi Adth	John 8:58; 10:30
182. Isa 9:6	The Prince of Peace, Sar Shalom	John 16:33
183. Isa 9:7	To establish an everlasting kingdom	Luke 1:32-33
184. Isa 9:7	His Character-Just	John 5:30
185. Isa 9:7	No end to his Government, Throne, and Peace	Luke 1:32-33
186. Isa 11:1	Called a Nazarene-the Branch	Matt 2:23
187. Isa 11:1	A rod out of Jesse-Son of Jesse	Luke 3:23-32
188. Isa 11:2	Anointed One by the Spirit	Matt 3:16-17; Acts 10:38
189. Isa 11:2	His Character-Wisdom, Knowledge, et al	Col 2:3
190. Isa 11:3	He would know their thoughts	Luke 6:8; John 2:25
191. Isa 11:4	Judge in righteousness	Acts 17:31
192. Isa 11:4	Judges with the sword of His mouth	Rev 2:16; 19:11, 15

©2010, 2012. Wheaton Press™ All Rights Reserved.

Life of Christ

Prophecy	Description	Fulfillment
193. Isa 11:5	Character: Righteous & Faithful	Rev 19:11
194. Isa 11:10	The Gentiles seek Him	John 12:18-21
195. Isa 12:2	Called Jesus-Yeshua	Matt 1:21
196. Isa 22:22	The One given all authority to govern	Rev 3:7
197. Isa 25:8	The Resurrection predicted	1 Cor 15:54
198. Isa 26:19	His power of Resurrection predicted	Matt 27:50-54
199. Isa 28:16	The Messiah is the precious corner stone	Acts 4:11-12
200. Isa 28:16	The Sure Foundation	1 Cor 3:11; Matt 16:18
201. Isa 29:13	He indicated hypocritical obedience to His Word	Matt 15:7-9
202. Isa 29:14	The wise are confounded by the Word	1 Cor 1:18-31
203. Isa 32:2	A Refuge-A man shall be a hiding place	Matt 23:37
204. Isa 35:4	He will come and save you	Matt 1:21
205. Isa 35:5-6	To have a ministry of miracles	Matt 11:2-6
206. Isa 40:3-4	Preceded by forerunner	John 1:23
207. Isa 40:9	"Behold your God"	John 1:36; 19:14
208. Isa 40:10	He will come to reward	Rev 22:12
209. Isa 40:11	A shepherd-compassionate life-giver	John 10:10-18
210. Isa 42:1-4	The Servant-as a faithful, patient redeemer	Matt 12:18-21
211. Isa 42:2	Meek and lowly	Matt 11:28-30
212. Isa 42:3	He brings hope for the hopeless	John 4
213. Isa 42:4	The nations shall wait on His teachings	John 12:20-26
214. Isa 42:6	The Light (salvation) of the Gentiles	Luke 2:32
215. Isa 42:1-6	His is a worldwide compassion	Matt 28:19-20
216. Isa 42:7	Blind eyes opened	John 9:25-38
217. Isa 43:11	He is the only Savior	Acts 4:12
218. Isa 44:3	He will send the Spirit of God	John 16:7-13
219. Isa 45:21-25	He is Lord and Savior	Phil 3:20; Titus 2:13
220. Isa 45:23	He will be the Judge	John 5:22; Rom 14:11
221. Isa 46:9-10	Declares things not yet done	John 13:19
222. Isa 48:12	The First and the Last	John 1:30; Rev 1:8, 17
223. Isa 48:16-17	He came as a Teacher	John 3:2
224. Isa 49:1	Called from the womb-His humanity	Matt 1:18
225. Isa 49:5	A Servant from the womb	Luke 1:31; Phil 2:7

 ©2010, 2012. Wheaton Press™ All Rights Reserved.

Prophecy	Description	Fulfillment
226. Isa 49:6	He will restore Israel	Acts 3:19-21; 15:16-17
227. Isa 49:6	He is Salvation for Israel	Luke 2:29-32
228. Isa 49:6	He is the Light of the Gentiles	John 8:12; Acts 13:47
229. Isa 49:6	He is Salvation unto the ends of the earth	Acts 15:7-18
230. Isa 49:7	He is despised of the Nation	John 1:11; 8:48-49; 19:14-15
231. Isa 50:3	Heaven is clothed in black at His humiliation	Luke 23:44-45
232. Isa 50:4	He is a learned counselor for the weary	Matt 7:29; 11:28-29
233. Isa 50:5	The Servant bound willingly to obedience	Matt 26:39
234. Isa 50:6a	"I gave my back to those who struck Me"	Matt 27:26
235. Isa 50:6b	He was smitten on the cheeks	Matt 26:67
236. Isa 50:6c	He was spat upon	Matt 27:30
237. Isa 52:7	Published good tidings upon mountains	Matt 5:12; 15:29; 28:16
238. Isa 52:13	The Servant exalted	Acts 1:8-11; Eph 1:19-22; Phil 2:5-9
239. Isa 52:14	The Servant shockingly abused	Luke 18:31-34; Matt 26:67-68
240. Isa 52:15	Nations startled by message of the Servant	Luke 18:31-34; Matt 26:67-68
241. Isa 52:15	His blood shed sprinkles nations	Heb 9:13-14; Rev 1:5
242. Isa 53:1	His people would not believe Him	John 12:37-38
243. Isa 53:2	Appearance of an ordinary man	Phil 2:6-8
244. Isa 53:3a	Despised	Luke 4:28-29
245. Isa 53:3b	Rejected	Matt 27:21-23
246. Isa 53:3c	Great sorrow and grief	Matt 26:37-38; Luke 19:41; Heb 4:15
247. Isa 53:3d	Men hide from being associated with Him	Mark 14:50-52
248. Isa 53:4a	He would have a healing ministry	Matt 8:16-17
249. Isa 53:4b	Thought to be cursed by God	Matt 26:66; 27:41-43
250. Isa 53:5a	Bears penalty for mankind's iniquities	2 Cor 5:21; Heb 2:9
251. Isa 53:5b	His sacrifice provides peace between man and God	Col 1:20
252. Isa 53:5c	His sacrifice would heal man of sin	1 Pet 2:24
253. Isa 53:6a	He would be the sin-bearer for all mankind	1 John 2:2; 4:10
254. Isa 53:6b	God's will that He bear sin for all mankind	Gal 1:4
255. Isa 53:7a	Oppressed and afflicted	Matt 27:27-31
256. Isa 53:7b	Silent before his accusers	Matt 27:12-14
257. Isa 53:7c	Sacrificial lamb	John 1:29; 1 Pet 1:18-19
258. Isa 53:8a	Confined and persecuted	Matt 26:47-27:31

©2010, 2012. Wheaton Press™ All Rights Reserved.

Life of Christ

Prophecy	Description	Fulfillment
259. Isa 53:8b	He would be judged	John 18:13-22
260. Isa 53:8c	Killed	Matt 27:35
261. Isa 53:8d	Dies for the sins of the world	1 John 2:2
262. Isa 53:9a	Buried in a rich man's grave	Matt 27:57
263. Isa 53:9b	Innocent and had done no violence	Luke 23:41; John 18:38
264. Isa 53:9c	No deceit in his mouth	1 Pet 2:22
265. Isa 53:10a	God's will that He die for mankind	John 18:11
266. Isa 53:10b	An offering for sin	Matt 20:28; Gal 3:13
267. Isa 53:10c	Resurrected and live forever	Rom 6:9
268. Isa 53:10d	He would prosper	John 17:1-5
269. Isa 53:11a	God fully satisfied with His suffering	John 12:27
270. Isa 53:11b	God's servant would justify man	Rom 5:8-9, 18-19
271. Isa 53:11c	The sin-bearer for all mankind	Heb 9:28
272. Isa 53:12a	Exalted by God because of his sacrifice	Matt 28:18
273. Isa 53:12b	He would give up his life to save mankind	Luke 23:46
274. Isa 53:12c	Numbered with the transgressors	Mark 15:27-28
275. Isa 53:12d	Sin-bearer for all mankind	1 Pet 2:24
276. Isa 53:12e	Intercede to God in behalf of mankind	Luke 23:34; Rom 8:34
277. Isa 55:3	Resurrected by God	Acts 13:34
278. Isa 55:4a	A witness	John 18:37
279. Isa 55:4b	He is a leader and commander	Heb 2:10
280. Isa 55:5	God would glorify Him	Acts 3:13
281. Isa 59:16a	Intercessor between man and God	Matt 10:32
282. Isa 59:16b	He would come to provide salvation	John 6:40
283. Isa 59:20	He would come to Zion as their Redeemer	Luke 2:38
284. Isa 60:1-3	He would show light to the Gentiles	Acts 26:23
285. Isa 61:1a	The Spirit of God upon him	Matt 3:16-17
286. Isa 61:1b	The Messiah would preach the good news	Luke 4:16-21
287. Isa 61:1c	Provide freedom from the bondage of sin	John 8:31-36
288. Isa 61:1-2a	Proclaim a period of grace	Gal 4:4-5
289. Jer 23:5-6	Descendant of David	Luke 3:23-31
290. Jer 23:5-6	The Messiah would be both God and Man	John 13:13; 1 Tim 3:16
291. Jer 31:22	Born of a virgin	Matt 1:18-20

 ©2010, 2012. Wheaton Press™ All Rights Reserved.

Prophecy	Description	Fulfillment
292. Jer 31:31	The Messiah would be the new covenant	Matt 26:28
293. Jer 33:14-15	Descendant of David	Luke 3:23-31
294. Ezek 34:23-24	Descendant of David	Matt 1:1
295. Ezek 37:24-25	Descendant of David	Luke 1:31-33
296. Dan 2:44-45	The Stone that shall break the kingdoms	Matt 21:44
297. Dan 7:13-14a	He would ascend into heaven	Acts 1:9-11
298. Dan 7:13-14b	Highly exalted	Eph 1:20-22
299. Dan 7:13-14c	His dominion would be everlasting	Luke 1:31-33
300. Dan 9:24a	To make an end to sins	Gal 1:3-5
301. Dan 9:24a	To make reconciliation for iniquity	Rom 5:10; 2 Cor 5:18-21
302. Dan 9:24b	He would be holy	Luke 1:35
303. Dan 9:25	His announcement	John 12:12-13
304. Dan 9:26a	Cut off	Matt 16:21; 21:38-39
305. Dan 9:26b	Die for the sins of the world	Heb 2:9
306. Dan 9:26c	Killed before the destruction of the temple	Matt 27:50-51
307. Dan 10:5-6	Messiah in a glorified state	Rev 1:13-16
308. Hos 11:1	He would be called out of Egypt	Matt 2:15
309. Hos 13:14	He would defeat death	1 Cor 15:55-57
310. Joel 2:32	Offer salvation to all mankind	Rom 10:9-13
311. Jonah 1:17	Death and resurrection of Christ	Matt 12:40; 16:4
312. Mic 5:2a	Born in Bethlehem	Matt 2:1-6
313. Mic 5:2b	Ruler in Israel	Luke 1:33
314. Mic 5:2c	From everlasting	John 8:58
315. Hag 2:6-9	He would visit the second Temple	Luke 2:27-32
316. Hag 2:23	Descendant of Zerubbabel	Luke 2:27-32
317. Zech 3:8	God's servant	John 17:4
318. Zech 6:12-13	Priest and King	Heb 8:1
319. Zech 9:9a	Greeted with rejoicing in Jerusalem	Matt 21:8-10
320. Zech 9:9b	Beheld as King	John 12:12-13
321. Zech 9:9c	The Messiah would be just	John 5:30
322. Zech 9:9d	The Messiah would bring salvation	Luke 19:10
323. Zech 9:9e	The Messiah would be humble	Matt 11:29
324. Zech 9:9f	Presented to Jerusalem riding on a donkey	Matt 21:6-9

©2010, 2012. Wheaton Press™ All Rights Reserved.

Prophecy	Description	Fulfillment
325. Zech 10:4	The cornerstone	Eph 2:20
326. Zech 11:4-6a	At His coming, Israel to have unfit leaders	Matt 23:1-4
327. Zech 11:4-6b	Rejection causes God to remove His protection	Luke 19:41-44
328. Zech 11:4-6c	Rejected in favor of another king	John 19:13-15
329. Zech 11:7	Ministry to "poor," the believing remnant	Matt 9:35-36
330. Zech 11:8a	Unbelief forces Messiah to reject them	Matt 23:33
331. Zech 11:8b	Despised	Matt 27:20
332. Zech 11:9	Stops ministering to those who rejected Him	Matt 13:10-11
333. Zech 11:10-11a	Rejection causes God to remove protection	Luke 19:41-44
334. Zech 11:10-11b	The Messiah would be God	John 14:7
335. Zech 11:12-13a	Betrayed for thirty pieces of silver	Matt 26:14-15
336. Zech 11:12-13b	Rejected	Matt 26:14-15
337. Zech 11:12-13c	Thirty pieces of silver cast in the house of the Lord	Matt 27:3-5
338. Zech 11:12-13d	The Messiah would be God	John 12:45
339. Zech 12:10a	The Messiah's body would be pierced	John 19:34-37
340. Zech 12:10b	The Messiah would be both God and man	John 10:30
341. Zech 12:10c	The Messiah would be rejected	John 1:11
342. Zech 13:7a	God's will He die for mankind	John 18:11
343. Zech 13:7b	A violent death	Mark 14:27
344. Zech 13:7c	Both God and man	John 14:9
345. Zech 13:7d	Israel scattered as a result of rejecting Him	Matt 26:31-56
346. Zech 14:4	He would return to the Mt. of Olives	Acts 1:11-12
347. Mal 3:1a	Messenger to prepare the way for Messiah	Mark 1:1-8
348. Mal 3:1b	Sudden appearance at the temple	Mark 11:15-16
349. Mal 3:1c	Messenger of the new covenant	Luke 4:43
350. Mal 4:5	Forerunner in spirit of Elijah	Matt 3:1-3; 11:10-14; 17:11-13
351. Mal 4:6	Forerunner would turn many to righteousness	Luke 1:16-17

 ©2010, 2012. Wheaton Press™ All Rights Reserved.

Prophecy Project Collaboration
Part I. Personal Reflection

Identify 5 matches you find most interesting or compelling.

1.

2.

3.

4.

5.

After identifying your five matches, respond to the questions below:

1. Explain the five passages you chose. Why did you choose those five, and how do they affect your perception of Christ as the Messiah?

2. What does God reveal about the Messiah through the verses highlighted in your discussion?

3. What have you learned or been challenged by through this project?

4. Explain the statement, "Jesus is central to all of Scripture."

5. How would your reading of God's Word change if Jesus became the center of everything in Scripture?

©2010, 2012. Wheaton Press™ All Rights Reserved.

Is Jesus the Messiah?
Examine for yourself

Some of the prophecies about the coming Messiah:

- Compare Genesis 9:26–27 with Luke 3:35.

    Out of the three sons of Noah, the Messiah would come through …

- Read Genesis 12:2–3, 22:18.

    Out of the descendants of Shem, the Messiah would come through …

- Read Genesis 21:12.

    Out of the two sons of Abraham, the Messiah would come through …

- Read Genesis 35:10–12 and Numbers 24:17.

    Out of the twelve sons of Jacob, the Messiah would come not through Joseph but through…

- Read Genesis 49:10, Psalm 78:67–68, and Isaiah 11:1–2.

    Out of the descendants of Judah, all would be rejected except for the family of …

- Read Jeremiah 23:5.

    Out of all of the sons of Jesse, all would be passed over except for …

    In other words, the Messiah would be the one who was the son of _____, the son of _____, the son of _____, the son of _____, the son of _____, the son of _____, the son of _____. It is as if the Bible gives us the exact address for the Messiah

    Read Matthew 1 together out loud. Write out your reflection on what you see regarding the "address" of the Messiah in comparison with the prophecies from the Old Testament.

 ©2010, 2012. Wheaton Press™ All Rights Reserved.

The forbidden chapter
Isaiah 53, TLB

[1]But, oh, how few believe it! Who will listen? To whom will God reveal his saving power? [2]In God's eyes he was like a tender green shoot, sprouting from a root in dry and sterile ground. But in our eyes there was no attractiveness at all, nothing to make us want him. [3]We despised him and rejected him—a man of sorrows, acquainted with bitterest grief. We turned our backs on him and looked the other way when he went by. He was despised, and we didn't care.

[4]Yet it was our grief he bore, our sorrows that weighed him down. And we thought his troubles were a punishment from God, for his own sins! [5]But he was wounded and bruised for our sins. He was beaten that we might have peace; he was lashed—and we were healed! [6]We—every one of us—have strayed away like sheep! We, who left God's paths to follow our own. Yet God laid on him the guilt and sins of every one of us!

[7]He was oppressed and he was afflicted, yet he never said a word. He was brought as a lamb to the slaughter; and as a sheep before her shearers is dumb, so he stood silent before the ones condemning him. [8]From prison and trial they led him away to his death. But who among the people of that day realized it was their sins that he was dying for—that he was suffering their punishment? [9]He was buried like a criminal, but in a rich man's grave; but he had done no wrong and had never spoken an evil word.

[10]But it was the Lord's good plan to bruise him and fill him with grief. However, when his soul has been made an offering for sin, then he shall have a multitude of children, many heirs. He shall live again, and God's program shall prosper in his hands.

[11]And when he sees all that is accomplished by the anguish of his soul, he shall be satisfied; and because of what he has experienced, my righteous Servant shall make many to be counted righteous before God, for he shall bear all their sins. [12]Therefore, I will give him the honors of one who is mighty and great because he has poured out his soul unto death. He was counted as a sinner, and he bore the sins of many, and he pled with God for sinners.

©2010, 2012. Wheaton Press™ All Rights Reserved.

Essential Question

Did Jesus fulfill the Old Testament prophecies regarding the future Messiah in the book of Isaiah?

Learning Goal

To articulate understanding and application of the concept of the fullness of Christ

Part I. Prophecy project

Directions:

Students will identify five compelling prophecies that were fulfilled by Christ and create a one–page prophecy reflection paper.

Part II. Prophecy project reflection paper
Purpose:

Students will use this paper to demonstrate an understanding of the concepts and application of Jesus as the Messiah and as the fulfillment of Old Testament prophecy.

- Students will demonstrate understanding of the concepts articulated through the assigned reading, the classroom lectures, and the classroom prophecy project.

- Students will demonstrate personal application and reflection of the concepts uncovered through the prophecy project, reading, lectures, and dialogue in class.

Directions:

Write a one–page reflection paper that demonstrates your understanding of the concept of Christ as the fulfillment of Old Testament prophecy and answer the four questions below, using the guidelines for a one–page paper. Please attach your completed prophecy project (work from class) to your one–page reflection paper.

A.   Which prophecies (if any) were most compelling, convincing, and convicting for you?

B.   In what ways did this project make the Bible more reliable or authoritative for you?

C.   What could your response be to someone who claims Jesus simply manipulated His life in such a way that He would fulfill all the Old Testament prophesies?

D.   How is the central theme of Scripture centered on the revelation of Jesus?

#Divine

Life of Christ

Unit Essential Questions

1. What do other religions teach about the divinity of Christ?

2. Did Jesus claim to be God?

3. Is it possible for Jesus to have been just a good man?

Unit Learning Objectives

A. To examine other religions and worldviews to learn their perspective on the divinity of Christ

B. To examine Scripture to discern if Jesus claimed to be the one and only God

C. To evaluate Jewish customs, traditions, and language to better understand the words and actions of Christ in the context of His generation and culture

D. To logically work through the process of whether or not it is possible for Christ to have simply been a good man

Unit Learning Assessments

1. Unit exam

Daily Essential Questions

1. Why does it matter whether or not Jesus was fully divine?

2. What do other religions believe about the divinity of Jesus Christ?

3. Did Jesus claim to be God?

4. Why was Jesus crucified?

5. What is significant about the word *Elohim*?

6. What does John 16–21 reveal about Christ?

 ©2010, 2012. Wheaton Press™ All Rights Reserved.

Bell Ringers
Reflect and Respond

1. If Jesus is who He said He is, then what difference does that make in my life?

1. Why does it matter if Jesus was fully divine?

1. How would a lack of full divinity affect Christ's roles from the tri–perspective view? What would be the implications on each role?

- Prophet:

- Priest:

- King:

2. At what point did Jesus become fully divine?

   How would you prove your answer from Scripture?

Notes and Discussion

©2010, 2012. Wheaton Press™ All Rights Reserved.

Is Jesus fully divine?
Notes and Discussion

 ©2010, 2012. Wheaton Press™ All Rights Reserved.

What do other religions believe and teach about the divinity of Christ?
Notes and Discussion

- Scientology

- Jehovah's Witnesses

- Mormonism

- Unitarian Universalism

©2010, 2012. Wheaton Press™ All Rights Reserved.

What do other religions believe and teach about the divinity of Christ?
Notes and Discussion

- Liberal and Emergent 'Christians'

- Arianism

- Buddhism

- Islam

- Hinduism

©2010, 2012. Wheaton Press™ All Rights Reserved.

Did Jesus claim to be God?
Small Group Project

Part 1. Passage study: Mark 14:60–64

A. What is the context surrounding the passage?

A. What does Jesus say?

A. What does it mean?

A. How do people respond?

B. What does it mean?

A. What additional cross references or research do you need to understand the passage?

Part II. Class Notes and Discussion

©2010, 2012. Wheaton Press™ All Rights Reserved.

Did Jesus claim to be God?
Small Group Project

Part I. Passage study: John 8:58–59

A. What is the context surrounding the passage?

A. What does Jesus say?

B. What does it mean?

C. How do people respond?

D. What does it mean?

A. What additional cross references or research do you need to understand the passage?

Part II. Class Notes and Discussion

 ©2010, 2012. Wheaton Press™ All Rights Reserved.

Did Jesus claim to be God?
Small Group Project

Part I. Passage study: John 10:30–31

A. What is the context surrounding the passage?

A. What does Jesus say?

B. What does it mean?

C. How do people respond?

D. What does it mean?

A. What additional cross references or research do you need to understand the passage?

Part II. Class Notes and Discussion

©2010, 2012. Wheaton Press™ All Rights Reserved.

What is some additional evidence that reveals Jesus claimed to be God?
Notes and Discussion

 ©2010, 2012. Wheaton Press™ All Rights Reserved.

What is some additional evidence that reveals Jesus claimed to be God?
Notes and Discussion

©2010, 2012. Wheaton Press™ All Rights Reserved.

If Jesus claimed to be God, then could He have been just a good man?
Notes and Discussion

Reflections from C.S. Lewis and the trilemma

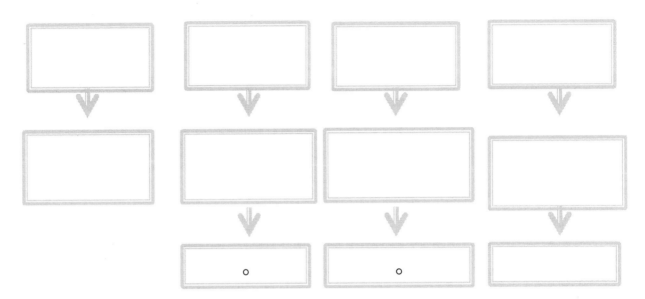

 ©2010, 2012. Wheaton Press™ All Rights Reserved.

What does John 16–21 reveal about Christ?
Notes and Discussion

©2010, 2012. Wheaton Press™ All Rights Reserved. 71

Gospel Check Insights
Notes and Discussion

 ©2010, 2012. Wheaton Press™ All Rights Reserved.

#Human

Life of Christ

Unit Essential Questions

1. Was Jesus fully human?

2. What do other religions believe about the humanity of Christ?

3. How does the full humanity of Christ influence my relationship with Jesus?

Unit Learning Objectives

A. To examine other religions and worldviews to learn their perspective on the humanity of Christ

B. To examine Scripture to discern if Jesus was fully human

C. To valuate historic and modern Gnosticism in light of the Epistles and church history

D. To examine Christ's relationship with the Holy Spirit as the model of a normal life

Unit Learning Assessments

1. Unit exam

Daily Essential Questions

1. Was Jesus fully human?

2. What is Gnosticism?

3. What is the *kenosis* and why does it matter?

4. If Jesus was fully human, how could he live a perfect life?

 ©2010, 2012. Wheaton Press™ All Rights Reserved.

Why does it matter whether or not Jesus was fully human?

Notes and Discussion

©2010, 2012. Wheaton Press™ All Rights Reserved.

What are some of the heresies regarding the humanity of Christ?

Notes and Discussion

 ©2010, 2012. Wheaton Press™ All Rights Reserved.

Was Jesus fully human?
Small Group Project

Passage study: 1 John 1, NASB

Introduction, the Incarnate Word

[1]What was from the beginning, what we have heard, what we have seen with our eyes, what we have looked at and touched with our hands, concerning the Word of Life—

[2]and the life was manifested, and we have seen and testify and proclaim to you the eternal life, which was with the Father and was manifested to us—

[3]what we have seen and heard we proclaim to you also, so that you too may have fellowship with us; and indeed our fellowship is with the Father, and with His Son Jesus Christ.

[4]These things we write, so that our joy may be made complete.

God Is Light

[5]This is the message we have heard from Him and announce to you, that God is Light, and in Him there is no darkness at all.

[6]If we say that we have fellowship with Him and yet walk in the darkness, we lie and do not practice the truth;

[7]but if we walk in the Light as He Himself is in the Light, we have fellowship with one another, and the blood of Jesus His Son cleanses us from all sin.

[8]If we say that we have no sin, we are deceiving ourselves and the truth is not in us.

[9]If we confess our sins, He is faithful and righteous to forgive us our sins and to cleanse us from all unrighteousness.

[10]If we say that we have not sinned, we make Him a liar and His word is not in us.

Observations

A. What is the context of the passage?
B. What does John say?
C. What does it mean?
D. Why is it significant?

©2010, 2012. Wheaton Press™ All Rights Reserved.

If Jesus was fully human, how could He live a perfect life?

Notes and Discussion

 ©2010, 2012. Wheaton Press™ All Rights Reserved.

#Atonement

Life of Christ

FROM FOLLOWER TO FRIEND

Unit Essential Questions

1. What physically happened to Jesus on the cross?

2. How does the cross of Christ fulfill the Old Testament requirements?

3. How are the perfect love and perfect wrath of God displayed through the cross of Christ?

Unit Learning Objectives

A. To examine and understand essential doctrinal definitions and their practical applications

B. To examine and articulate how Christ's death perfectly fulfills the Old Testament sacrificial system

C. To examine and articulate how the perfect love and perfect wrath of God is displayed through the cross of Christ

D. To examine scriptural evidence to determine if Christ ever went to hell after He died

Unit Learning Assessments

1. Gospel Project appendix definitions

2. Love and wrath reflection paper

3. Atonement assessment

Daily Essential Questions

1. What physically happened to Christ on the cross?

2. What spiritually happened through the sacrifice of Christ on the cross?

3. What theologically happened through the atoning work of Christ?

4. How are the perfect love and perfect wrath of God fulfilled through the death of Christ on the cross?

5. Did Jesus go to hell after He died?

 ©2010, 2012. Wheaton Press™ All Rights Reserved.

What physically happened to Jesus on the cross?

Notes and Discussion

What theologically happened through the atoning work of Christ?

Notes and Discussion

Name the seven essential truths to understanding the significance of Christ's death on the cross. **NOTE: You must state the references.

1.

2.

3.

4.

5.

6.

7.

 ©2010, 2012. Wheaton Press™ All Rights Reserved.

What theologically happened through the atoning work of Christ?

Define the following doctrines and theological words:

1. Justification:

2. Sanctification:

3. Reconciliation:

4. Substitution:

5. Scapegoat:

6. Propitiation:

7. Day of Atonement:

©2010, 2012. Wheaton Press™ All Rights Reserved.

What theologically happened through the atoning work of Christ?

Define the following doctrines and theological words:

8. Penal substitutionary atonement:

9. Forbearance:

10. Expiation:

11. Atonement:

12. Imputation:

13. Glorification:

 ©2010, 2012. Wheaton Press™ All Rights Reserved.

What theologically happened through the atoning work of Christ?
Short Answer

What are the three ways that Paul used the word *saved* in the New Testament?
(Identify the terms and their meanings.)

1.

2.

3.

Did Jesus go to hell when He died?

1.

2.

3.

4.

5.

©2010, 2012. Wheaton Press™ All Rights Reserved.

Did Jesus go to hell when He died?
Short Answer

Small group project

Reason 1:

Reason 2:

Reason 3:

Reason 4:

Reason 5:

Notes and Discussion

 ©2010, 2012. Wheaton Press™ All Rights Reserved.

How did Christ's death fulfill the Old Testament sacrificial system?

Notes and Discussion

©2010, 2012. Wheaton Press™ All Rights Reserved. 87

Jesus died for our sins, but what else did the cross accomplish?

Notes and Discussion

 ©2010, 2012. Wheaton Press™ All Rights Reserved.

What does Luke reveal about the atonement of Christ?

Notes and Discussion

©2010, 2012. Wheaton Press™ All Rights Reserved. 89

Practical Scenario 1

A friend invites you to a local coffee shop and asks you the following question:
"How is it fair that God can put both my really nice neighbor and Adolf Hitler side by side in hell?"

Using what you have learned in this unit, write out your response.

Notes and Discussion

 ©2010, 2012. Wheaton Press™ All Rights Reserved.

Practical Scenario II

A friend invites you to a local coffee shop and asks you the following question:
"How can a loving God send people to hell?"

Using what you have learned in this unit, write out your response.

Notes and Discussion

©2010, 2012. Wheaton Press™ All Rights Reserved.

How are the perfect love and perfect wrath of God displayed through the cross of Christ?

Notes and Discussion

 ©2010, 2012. Wheaton Press™ All Rights Reserved.

Gospel Check Insights
Notes and Discussion

©2010, 2012. Wheaton Press™ All Rights Reserved.   93

Gospel Check Insights
Notes and Discussion

 ©2010, 2012. Wheaton Press™ All Rights Reserved.

#Resurrected

Life of Christ

Unit Essential Questions

1. What evidence exists that Jesus actually rose from the dead?

2. How does my perspective or conviction about the resurrection influence my relationship with Jesus?

Unit Learning Objectives

A. To examine the biblical evidence that Jesus rose from the dead

B. To examine the circumstantial evidence that Jesus rose from the dead

C. To examine the secular historical evidence that Jesus rose from the dead

D. To articulate a reasoned apologetic of personal beliefs regarding the resurrection of Christ

Unit Learning Assessments

1. 9 Proofs project

2. 9 Proofs reflection paper

Daily Essential Questions

1. What do I believe about the resurrection of Christ from the dead?

2. Is it reasonable to believe that Jesus rose from the dead?

3. What evidence exists that Jesus rose from the dead?

4. What do I believe is reasonable about the resurrection?

5. Can I articulate a clear apologetic for the resurrection of Christ from the dead?

 ©2010, 2012. Wheaton Press™ All Rights Reserved.

Did Jesus rise from the dead?

Notes and Discussion

What do I believe about the resurrection of Christ?

Why do I believe what I believe? (What proof or evidence is my belief based upon?)

What does Jesus prove or accomplish through His resurrection?

If Jesus did not rise from the dead, what would be the effect on modern Christianity?

Why does the resurrection of Christ matter?
Arguments from Scripture and logic

Notes and Discussion

 ©2010, 2012. Wheaton Press™ All Rights Reserved.

Did Jesus rise from the dead?
What are the competing theories about the resurrection of Christ?

Notes and Discussion

©2010, 2012. Wheaton Press™ All Rights Reserved. 99

What is the biblical evidence for the resurrection of Christ?
Examining the biblical evidence

Directions: Summarize each of the nine pieces of biblical evidence for the resurrection of Christ. Include at least one Scripture reference within each summary.

1.

2.

3.

4.

 ©2010, 2012. Wheaton Press™ All Rights Reserved.

What is the biblical evidence for the resurrection of Christ?
Examining the biblical evidence

5.

6.

7.

8.

9.

What is the circumstantial evidence for the resurrection of Christ?
Examining the circumstantial evidence

Directions: Summarize each of the ten pieces of circumstantial evidence by answering all of the following three questions:

A. What is the claim?
B. Why is the claim significant?
C. How does the claim give credible evidence for an argument?

1.
   A.

   B.

   C.

2.
   A.

   B.

   C.

3.
   A.

   B.

   C.

4.
   A.

   B.

   C.

5.
   A.

   B.

   C.

    ©2010, 2012. Wheaton Press™ All Rights Reserved.

What is the circumstantial evidence for the resurrection of Christ?

Examining the circumstantial evidence

6.

    A.

    B.

    C.

7.

    A.

    B.

    C.

8.

    A.

    B.

    C.

9.

    A.

    B.

    C.

10.

    A.

    B.

    C.

©2010, 2012. Wheaton Press™ All Rights Reserved.

What is the non-Christian historical evidence for the resurrection of Christ?
Examining the secular historical evidence

Directions: Summarize each of the pieces of non-Christian historical evidence for the resurrection of Christ.

1.

2.

3.

4.

 ©2010, 2012. Wheaton Press™ All Rights Reserved.

What do I find to be the most reasonable evidence for the resurrection?

What do I believe? Why do I believe it?

Directions: From your perspective, what are the three most reasonable pieces of evidence in each category?

What is the biblical evidence for the resurrection of Christ?

1.

2.

3.

What is the circumstantial evidence for the resurrection of Christ?

1.

2.

3.

What is the secular, historical evidence for the resurrection of Christ?

1.

2.

3.

©2010, 2012. Wheaton Press™ All Rights Reserved.

Nine proofs for the resurrection of Christ

What do I believe? Why do I believe it?

Assessment:

Directions: Answer the following question in a well-formatted, five-paragraph answer. Each paragraph must have a minimum of four sentences. The first paragraph should be a well crafted introduction and the last paragraph should be a smoothly-articulated conclusion.

Question: Based on biblical, historical, secular, and circumstantial evidence, did Jesus die and rise from the dead?

 ©2010, 2012. Wheaton Press™ All Rights Reserved.

Gospel Check Insights
Notes and Discussion

©2010, 2012. Wheaton Press™ All Rights Reserved.   107

Gospel Check Insights
Notes and Discussion

 ©2010, 2012. Wheaton Press™ All Rights Reserved.

#Returning

Life of Christ

FROM FOLLOWER TO FRIEND

Unit Essential Questions

1. How does the life of Christ fit into the eternal plan of God?

2. What does the Bible tell us about the return of Christ?

3. Where is Jesus now, and what will He do when He returns?

4. How does my perspective of Christ's return influence my relationship with Christ and others?

Unit Learning Objectives

A. To examine what the Bible says about the current and future ministry of Christ

B. To examine primary orthodox perspectives on the return of Christ

C. To understand the significance of modern events in light of biblical prophecy regarding Christ's return

D. To examine my role in the eternal mission of God in light of the return of Christ

Unit Learning Assessments

1. Theological position paper

Daily Essential Questions

1. How does the life of Christ fit into the eternal plan of God?

2. Where is Jesus now?

3. How does the return of Christ fit into the eternal plan of God?

4. What will He do when He returns?

5. How should my beliefs affect my current life?

 ©201.0, 201.2. Wheaton Press™ All Rights Reserved.

Bell Ringers
Reflection and Discussion

Directions: Answer the following questions based on your opinion and understanding of Scripture

1. Where is Jesus today?

2. What Scripture do you have to support your answer for question 1?

3. Is Jesus reigning as king today? (Why or why not?)

4. What Scripture do you have to support your answer for 3?

5. What are the implications of your answers to these questions?

©2010, 2012. Wheaton Press™ All Rights Reserved.

Where is Jesus today?
Research project

Directions:

Find a partner. Have each partner summarize five of the ten statements with two or three bullet points. When finished, combine your lists to create a complete list of ten, which you will utilize as a study guide for this unit.

**NOTE: Your summaries need to contain answers to the following three questions:

- What does the Bible teach (and what do I believe about the subject)?

- Why should I, or do I, believe this? (What references or scriptural evidence do I base my belief upon?)

- So what? What are the implications of this belief for my life?

1.

2.

3.

 ©2010, 2012. Wheaton Press™ All Rights Reserved.

Where is Jesus today?
Research project

4.

5.

6.

7.

©2010, 2012. Wheaton Press™ All Rights Reserved.

Where is Jesus today?
Research project

8.

9.

10.

 ©2010, 2012. Wheaton Press™ All Rights Reserved.

What will Jesus do upon His return?
Research project

Directions:

Find a partner. Have each partner summarize five of the ten statements with two or three bullet points. When finished, combine your lists to create a complete list of 10, which you will utilize as a study guide for this unit.

NOTE: Your summaries need to contain the answers to the following three questions:

- What does the Bible teach (and what do I believe about the subject)?

- Why should I, or do I, believe this? (What references or scriptural evidence do I base my belief upon?)

- So what? What are the implications of this belief on my life?

     1.

     2.

     3.

What will Jesus do upon His return?
Research project

4.

5.

6.

7.

 ©2010, 2012. Wheaton Press™ All Rights Reserved.

What will Jesus do upon His return?
Research project

8.

9.

10.

©2010, 2012. Wheaton Press™ All Rights Reserved.

What will happen when Jesus returns?
Revelation 21–22, NASB

Observations

Chapter 21
The New Heaven and Earth

A. What is the context of the passage?
B. What does John say?
C. What does it mean?
D. Why is it significant?

[1]Then I saw a new heaven and a new earth; for the first heaven and the first earth passed away, and there is no longer any sea. [2]And I saw the holy city, new Jerusalem, coming down out of heaven from God, made ready as a bride adorned for her husband. [3]And I heard a loud voice from the throne, saying, "Behold, the tabernacle of God is among men, and He will dwell among them, and they shall be His people, and God Himself will be among them, [4]and He will wipe away every tear from their eyes; and there will no longer be any death; there will no longer be any mourning, or crying, or pain; the first things have passed away."

[5]And He who sits on the throne said, "Behold, I am making all things new." And He said, "Write, for these words are faithful and true." [6]Then He said to me, "It is done. I am the Alpha and the Omega, the beginning and the end. I will give to the one who thirsts from the spring of the water of life without cost. [7]He who overcomes will inherit these things, and I will be his God and he will be My son. [8]But for the cowardly and unbelieving and abominable and murderers and immoral persons and sorcerers and idolaters and all liars, their part will be in the lake that burns with fire and brimstone, which is the second death."

[9]Then one of the seven angels who had the seven bowls full of the seven last plagues came and spoke with me, saying, "Come here, I will show you the bride, the wife of the Lamb."

 ©2010, 2012. Wheaton Press™ All Rights Reserved.

What will happen when Jesus returns?
Revelation 21–22, NASB

The New Jerusalem

[10]And he carried me away in the Spirit to a great and high mountain, and showed me the holy city, Jerusalem, coming down out of heaven from God, [11]having the glory of God. Her brilliance was like a very costly stone, as a stone of crystal–clear jasper. [12]It had a great and high wall, with twelve gates, and at the gates twelve angels; and names were written on them, which are the names of the twelve tribes of the sons of Israel. [13]There were three gates on the east and three gates on the north and three gates on the south and three gates on the west. [14]And the wall of the city had twelve foundation stones, and on them were the twelve names of the twelve apostles of the Lamb.

[15]The one who spoke with me had a gold measuring rod to measure the city, and its gates and its wall. [16]The city is laid out as a square, and its length is as great as the width; and he measured the city with the rod, fifteen hundred miles; its length and width and height are equal. [17]And he measured its wall, seventy–two yards, according to human measurements, which are also angelic measurements. [18]The material of the wall was jasper; and the city was pure gold, like clear glass. [19]The foundation stones of the city wall were adorned with every kind of precious stone. The first foundation stone was jasper; the second, sapphire; the third, chalcedony; the fourth, emerald; [20]the fifth, sardonyx; the sixth, sardius; the seventh, chrysolite; the eighth, beryl; the ninth, topaz; the tenth, chrysoprase; the eleventh, jacinth; the twelfth, amethyst. [21]And the twelve gates were twelve pearls; each one of the gates was a single pearl. And the street of the city was pure gold, like transparent glass.

Observations

A. What is the context of the passage?
B. What does John say?
C. What does it mean?
D. Why is it significant?

What will happen when Jesus returns?
Revelation 21–22, NASB

Observations

A. What is the context of the passage?
B. What does John say?
C. What does it mean?
D. Why is it significant?

²²I saw no temple in it, for the Lord God the Almighty and the Lamb are its temple. ²³And the city has no need of the sun or of the moon to shine on it, for the glory of God has illumined it, and its lamp is the Lamb. ²⁴The nations will walk by its light, and the kings of the earth will bring their glory into it. ²⁵In the daytime (for there will be no night there) its gates will never be closed; ²⁶and they will bring the glory and the honor of the nations into it; ²⁷and nothing unclean, and no one who practices abomination and lying, shall ever come into it, but only those whose names are written in the Lamb's book of life.

Chapter 22
The River and the Tree of Life

¹Then he showed me a river of the water of life, clear as crystal, coming from the throne of God and of the Lamb, ²in the middle of its street. On either side of the river was the tree of life, bearing twelve kinds of fruit, yielding its fruit every month; and the leaves of the tree were for the healing of the nations. ³There will no longer be any curse; and the throne of God and of the Lamb will be in it, and His bond–servants will serve Him; ⁴they will see His face, and His name will be on their foreheads. ⁵And there will no longer be any night; and they will not have need of the light of a lamp nor the light of the sun, because the Lord God will illumine them; and they will reign forever and ever.

⁶And he said to me, "These words are faithful and true"; and the Lord, the God of the spirits of the prophets, sent His angel to show to His bond–servants the things which must soon take place.

⁷"And behold, I am coming quickly. Blessed is he who heeds the words of the prophecy of this book."

   ©2010, 2012. Wheaton Press™ All Rights Reserved.

What will happen when Jesus returns?
Revelation 21–22, NASB

⁸I, John, am the one who heard and saw these things. And when I heard and saw, I fell down to worship at the feet of the angel who showed me these things. ⁹But he said to me, "Do not do that. I am a fellow servant of yours and of your brethren the prophets and of those who heed the words of this book. Worship God."

The Final Message

¹⁰And he said to me, "Do not seal up the words of the prophecy of this book, for the time is near. ¹¹Let the one who does wrong, still do wrong; and the one who is filthy, still be filthy; and let the one who is righteous, still practice righteousness; and the one who is holy, still keep himself holy."

¹²"Behold, I am coming quickly, and My reward is with Me, to render to every man according to what he has done. ¹³I am the Alpha and the Omega, the first and the last, the beginning and the end."

¹⁴Blessed are those who wash their robes, so that they may have the right to the tree of life, and may enter by the gates into the city. ¹⁵Outside are the dogs and the sorcerers and the immoral persons and the murderers and the idolaters, and everyone who loves and practices lying.

¹⁶"I, Jesus, have sent My angel to testify to you these things for the churches. I am the root and the descendant of David, the bright morning star."

¹⁷The Spirit and the bride say, "Come." And let the one who hears say, "Come." And let the one who is thirsty come; let the one who wishes take the water of life without cost.

Observations

A. What is the context of the passage?
B. What does John say?
C. What does it mean?
D. Why is it significant?

©2010, 2012. Wheaton Press™ All Rights Reserved.

What will happen when Jesus returns?
Revelation 21–22, NASB

Observations

[18]I testify to everyone who hears the words of the prophecy of this book: if anyone adds to them, God will add to him the plagues which are written in this book; [19]and if anyone takes away from the words of the book of this prophecy, God will take away his part from the tree of life and from the holy city, which are written in this book.

[20]He who testifies to these things says, "Yes, I am coming quickly." Amen. Come, Lord Jesus.

[21]The grace of the Lord Jesus be with all. Amen.

A. What is the context of the passage?
B. What does John say?
C. What does it mean?
D. Why is it significant?

 ©2010, 2012. Wheaton Press™ All Rights Reserved.

Assessment of learning
Doctrine position paper

There are three stages for this assessment.

1. **Formative stage**: This the first draft of your position paper. It will not be graded, but will demonstrate your learning progression and process.

2. **Summative assessment**: This the final draft of your position paper. It is graded, and will demonstrate what you have learned.
**NOTE: Your last copy of a position paper becomes your summative assessment grade.

3. **Student-initiated assessment**: This demonstration of higher learning is initiated at any time during the process by a student who resubmits a formative position paper to demonstrate a higher level of learning. This ensures that throughout the process, learning is the constant and time is the variable.

Summative grading:

Learning objectives in the WHAT and WHY sections of the paper will be based on this scale of proficiency:

1	2	3	4
Demonstrates little (if any) knowledge or understanding of material explicitly taught in class. Zero to 50% of statements are backed up by outside references.	Demonstrates basic knowledge or understanding of material explicitly taught in class. 50% to 75% of statements are backed up by references.	Demonstrates knowledge or understanding of material explicitly taught in class and includes material explicitly taught in the course textbook. 75% to 90% of statements are backed up by references.	Demonstrates level 3 knowledge and understanding and includes material pulled from additional outside academic/theological resources or demonstrates higher–level critical thinking by connecting specific doctrines to other essential learning outcomes, essential questions, or doctrines. 90–100% of statements are backed up by outside references and sources.

0	1	2
Not Attempted	Student demonstrates a generic or simplistic application. Sentences or thoughts are not complete. Responses do not meet the minimum of four sentences for a complete paragraph. Student demonstrates basic (if any) interaction with the material in a personal way. Thoughts are generic or incomplete in nature.	Evidence is given that the student interacted with the significance of their beliefs in a meaningful way. References are made to how his or her beliefs or apologetic affect his or her life and demonstrate higher–level thought, critical thinking, and personal reflection. Thoughts are complete and demonstrate an interaction with the material in paragraphs of at least four sentences.

Assessment of learning
Doctrine position paper

Summative grading:

For every learning objective you will be assessed on what you <u>know</u>, <u>understand</u>, and <u>do</u> (K.U.D.) as a result of your interaction with the material. Each position paper will assess three areas of learning through a *What?*, *Why?*, and *So What?* section in your paper.

1. **What?** (doctrinal understanding)

   This section is a demonstration of what you <u>know</u> to be true (40%).

   Every sentence in this section must contain a reference. References are what separates an opinion paper from a position paper.

   Each sentence should contain the words, "I believe," followed by a statement of your beliefs, then followed by a reference.

2. **Why?** (doctrinal apologetic)

   This section is a demonstration of your <u>understanding</u> of the reason that you believe (see 1 Peter 3:15) (40%).

   While many of the sentences in this section will contain references, it is not mandatory that all of them contain references.

   Sentences should contain the words, "I believe (restatement of belief) because…" followed by the reason you find your belief to be reasonable. You cannot state that you believe something "because the Bible says so," because you are taking a position on why you have reached your conclusion.

3. **So What?** (practical application)

   This section is a demonstration of what you will <u>do</u> to apply your knowledge and understanding to your life beyond the classroom (20%).

   This section should be a reflection of your personality and writing style.

 ©2010, 2012. Wheaton Press™ All Rights Reserved.

#Respond

Life of Christ

FROM FOLLOWER TO FRIEND

Unit Essential Questions

1. What is worship?

2. What is my response to Jesus?

3. How will I articulate what I have learned to others?

Unit Learning Objectives

A. To articulate a personalized response to Christ's question, "who do others say that I am?"

Unit Learning Assessments

1. Gospel Project

2. Final presentation

3. Final exam

Daily Essential Questions

1. What is the meaning of worship?

2. What functional saviors compete for prominence in my life?

3. What will be my response to the invitation of Christ?

4. How will I articulate what I have learned?

 ©2010, 2012. Wheaton Press™ All Rights Reserved.

Reflection

Take some time to reflect on what you have been learning.

1. What has God been teaching me?

2. What have I learned through this process?

3. What is one surprise I've had?

4. What is one thing that stands out to me where I can see growth in my life?

5. What is one area where I would like to see more growth between now and the end of the semester?

©2010, 2012. Wheaton Press™ All Rights Reserved.

How will I respond?
Notes and Dialogue

1. What is worship?

2. Who or what do I glorify through my life and actions?

3. What makes Jesus superior to other saviors? Who or what do I trust to save me?

4. What is my response to Jesus?

 ©2010, 2012. Wheaton Press™ All Rights Reserved.

What is a functional savior?
Notes and Dialogue

How do functional saviors manifest themselves in my life?
Personal reflection

 ©2010, 2012. Wheaton Press™ All Rights Reserved.

#Resources

Life of Christ

How to Write a One–Page Paper for Bible Class

It is not enough to simply memorize Bible facts or acquire biblical knowledge. Students need to be given the opportunity to wrestle with important issues, develop personal beliefs, and articulate those beliefs in clear and convincing ways, in both written and oral form. At Wheaton Academy, we value the ability to think critically and communicate clearly about theological truth. It is the belief of the Bible Department that Bible class offers the opportunity to practice and develop these skills through the medium of one–page papers.

One–page papers are made up of a centered title and four critical paragraphs. The first part of the paper is referred to as the "hook" paragraph, and it is used to relate the topic to the audience. The second part of the paper is the "book" paragraph. The purpose of this paragraph is to clearly state the main concept of the paper. The third paragraph is the "look" paragraph, and it is where the writer illustrates the main point he or she has outlined in the second paragraph. The fourth and final section is called the "took" paragraph. It is in this final paragraph that the writer outlines a personal application, lesson, or "take away" from the topic.

Each individual paragraph must also contain a few key elements. One of the key elements is that each paragraph needs a minimum of four sentences. Another key element is that each paragraph needs to include transition sentences and be double–spaced. The paper should be written using either eleven- or twelve-point Times New Roman or Arial font. Finally, while the paper itself will using APA guidelines, it is important to note that the paper must not be longer than one page in total length (Bible Reference 1:1).

There are three main things you will accomplish through these papers. First, you will critically examine your personal beliefs. Second, you will learn how to communicate your beliefs in concise written form. Third and finally, you will have a collection of papers outlining your beliefs, which you can use for personal reference in the future.

 ©2010, 2012. Wheaton Press™ All Rights Reserved.

Student Name
Class, Period
Date.

Commentary on _____ (name of Gospel)

Chapter 1

Write a one-paragraph synopsis or reflection on each chapter. Each paragraph should include a single line identifying the chapter (see above). Each paragraph should start at least one space after the chapter heading, and each paragraph should have at least four sentences. Reflections on the passage could include summaries, devotional journal entries, or references to specific verses. If you reference a verse, do not quote the verse verbatim; instead, summarize or personalize the context or meaning and include an APA style reference at the end of the sentence (Gospel 1:1).

Chapter 2

Write a one-paragraph synopsis or reflection on each chapter. Each paragraph should include a single line identifying the chapter (see above). Each paragraph should start at least one space after the chapter heading, and each paragraph should have at least four sentences. Reflections on the passage could include summaries, devotional journal entries, or references to specific verses. If you reference a verse, do not quote the verse verbatim; instead, summarize or personalize the context or meaning and include an APA style reference at the end of the sentence (Gospel 1:1).

Chapter 3

Write a one-paragraph synopsis or reflection on each chapter. Each paragraph should include a single line identifying the chapter (see above). Each paragraph should start at least one space after the chapter heading, and each paragraph should have at least four sentences. Reflections on the passage could include summaries, devotional journal entries, or references to specific verses. If you reference a verse, do not quote the verse verbatim; instead, summarize or personalize the context or meaning and include an APA style reference at the end of the sentence (Gospel 1:1).

Gospel Project
Table of Contents

Table of Contents

PART I.   Commentary

Synopsis and reflection   3
Commentary on Matthew   4
Commentary on Luke   12
Commentary on John   17

PART II.   Appendix

A. Atonement definitions   28
B. Tri–perspective reflection paper   29
C. Prophecy project reflection paper   31
D. Perfect love and perfect wrath paper   33
E. Nine proofs apologetic paper   35
F. "Where is Jesus now?" position paper   39

    ©2010, 2012. Wheaton Press™ All Rights Reserved.

Gospel Check Insights
Notes and Discussion

©2010, 2012. Wheaton Press™ All Rights Reserved.

DUAL CREDIT FOR STUDENTS

Wheaton Press is excited to offer students the opportunity to receive dual credit for their Bible classes through a unique partnership with Colorado Christian University. Each Wheaton Press course has been recognized as the equivalent of a college-level class. As a result, Wheaton Press courses provide the opportunity for your students to receive dual credit.

Participating students will receive

• The opportunity to gain college credit during their normal course work at an affordable rate.

• College credits that are transferable to 90% of colleges and universities.*

About Colorado Christian University

• Colorado Christian University, a four-year Christian university located in Denver, Colorado, is fully accredited through the Higher Learning Commission of the North Central Association of Colleges and Schools.

• This means that credits are transferable to almost any school in the nation, including state universities and private colleges.

How students participate

When your students choose the dual-credit option they are able to earn three college credits for only $200 per class while they are taking their regular Bible Class.

Your students participate in the same assessments regardless of whether or not they participate. There is no extra work or assessments to receive the college credit in addition to the credit they will be receiving through your school.

This means that your students have the opportunity to enter college or university with up to 21 transferable college credits for only $1,400 over the course of four years.

Students pay the $200 course fee at the time of their registration at CCU. This course fee is paid directly to CCU and not to your school.

Students must earn a C or above to ensure that credit is valid at CCU or other colleges and universities.

*Note: Individual colleges and universities determine if they accept credit from Colorado Christian University.

In a recent survey conducted by CCU, over 90% of schools accepted their dual credit enrollment – including all public and private Christian universities surveyed.

Generally, the schools who did not accept their dual credit did not accept any form of college credit earned in high school – even AP credit.

Learn more at WheatonPress.com/DualCredit

 ©2010, 2012. Wheaton Press™ All Rights Reserved.

23238383R00076

Made in the USA
Columbia, SC
10 August 2018